the cinema of WIM WENDERS

DIRECTORS' CUTS

the cinema of
WIM WENDERS

the celluloid highway

alexander graf

WALLFLOWER PRESS LONDON & NEW YORK

First published in Great Britain in 2002 by
Wallflower Press
5 Pond Street, London NW3 2PN
www.wallflowerpress.co.uk

A catalogue for this book is available from the British Library

ISBN 1-903364-29-9 (paperback)
ISBN 1-903364-30-2 (hardback)

Book design by Rob Bowden Design

Printed in Great Britain by Antony Rowe, Chippenham, Wiltshire

CONTENTS

LIST OF ILLUSTRATIONS

ACKNOWLEDGEMENTS

Many thanks to all those who helped me put together the material for this book, especially Peter Mahler, Merten Worthmann, Alessandro di Todaro, Professor Dietrich Scheunemann, and the BFI.

A special thank you to Claudia Daseking at Road Movies for allowing me to use the pictures, and to In-Ah, who really does answer emails.

And a big thank you especially to Laura and my mother for their generosity, patience and understanding.

INTRODUCTION

Although a relative late-comer to the movement known as the *Neues deutsches Kino*, or New German Cinema, Wim Wenders is internationally its best known and most successful active member today. In a career spanning almost four decades, he has made eleven short films, seventeen feature films, seven documentaries, two television films, several music videos, and numerous advertising films for television, many of which have been awarded prizes at international film-festivals. His work as a photographer has been exhibited on eight separate occasions in Europe, Asia and America, and he has published nine books.

At first glance this diversity of theme, format and genre might make it difficult to identify areas of unity within Wenders' work. However, Wenders has been unusually and passionately vocal on questions regarding the cinematic medium. His self-reflexive, intellectual discourse betrays a preoccupation with a personal morality, or moral code, that he attaches to film and cinema, whether speaking of his own work or that of other film-makers or recognised film schools and traditions. This tendency is discernible not only in the themes and production methods of his films, but also in interviews and in his published volumes of writings and photographs. The theoretical question most consistently under discussion, and to which Wenders never appears to find an answer with which he is fully satisfied, has been the incompatibility, or conflict, that he perceives to exist between the film image and the filmic story – two elements of film that, together with sound, represent the aesthetic and technical basis of modern narrative cinema.

The nature of this problem is twofold: on one side, Wenders recognises that he has to meet his audience's demand for story in film in order to be commercially viable as an independent director (a precondition in commercial feature film production, as opposed to avant-garde or experimental film production). In a speech given in 1982 Wenders accounts for this audience demand for story as a universal human desire rather than as a personal attitude:

> Peoples' primary requirement is that some kind of coherence be provided. Stories give people the feeling that there is meaning, that there is ultimately an order lurking behind the incredible confusion of appearances and phenomena that surrounds them. This order is what people require more than anything else; yes, I would almost say that the notion of order or story is connected with the godhead. Stories are substitutes for God. Or maybe the other way round.[1]

Beyond commercial considerations, then, Wenders perceives stories to function as structures in which seemingly arbitrary or unrelated events or phenomena can acquire meaning because they are placed in a new relation to other events or phenomena within the same structure; or because stories can place these into the brace of a logical temporal continuity, which reassures the viewer that there is an order to the cacophony of visual and audio impressions it is exposed to in daily life. This conception of an order-bringing function inherent to stories has equal relevance for film production and for the filmic story.

On the other hand, Wenders is suspicious of story. He considers it an unstable element within film and attributes to it the potential to create a misbalance with the images in his films. He refers to his school film *Silver City* (1968) to illustrate the mechanism of this instability. *Silver City* consists of thirteen static shots, mostly filmed from the windows of various apartments that he had lived in during his time at the Munich Film and Television Academy (HFF). The film is markedly absent of action of any kind until the sixth shot, in which the intention was to film a train passing through a landscape. Just before the end of the sequence, however, a man enters the frame from the right, running across the rail-tracks, exiting left: a completely unplanned intervention of the coincidental which seems to have ruined the director's idea of the film. Wenders exclaims that the man running through the picture disrupted 'the peacefulness of the landscape with the train'.[2] The German publicist Norbert Grob claims to detect in Wenders' sceptical account of his accidental birth as a storyteller a fall from grace, that this was an early realisation that he would, from that moment on, be damned to tell stories in film even against his will.[3] In fact, Wenders' goal had been a pure observation of the scene, but the sudden intervention of the man crossing the tracks in front of the camera suggested the possible existence of a story on the edge of the frame, threatening to take over the meaning of the sequence because 'people would see entirely fanciful connections between scenes and interpret them as having narrative intentions'.[4]

The creation of a story against the will of the director, Wenders contends, is the first way in which story can dominate in a film. The second reason for his suspicious approach to story is related to the first: that the story, once it has forced its way into existence, can begin to build illusory connections between autonomous events or phenomena. The montage, or editing process, that enables several independent time-sequences to be projected consecutively, means that not only can individual images be placed into temporal connection with one another, but also that the sequences these build can have a relation to other, separate sequences of images, which alone is sufficient to generate or infer meaning not actually present in the images in an artificial manner. This is a process that Wenders considers to belong much more within the domain of writing, and to be unbefitting of images:

> For a writer, a story seems to be the logical end-product: words want to form sentences, and the sentences want to stand in some continuous discourse; a writer doesn't have to force the words into a sentence or the sentences into a story ... For me, images don't automatically lend themselves to be part of a story. If they're to function in the way that words and sentences do, they have to be 'forced' – that is, I have to manipulate them ... I dislike the manipulation that's necessary to press all the images of a film into one story ... In the relationship between story and image, I see the story as a kind of vampire, trying to suck all the blood from an image.[5]

Wenders' view, that stories bring out 'lies, nothing but lies, and the biggest lie is that they show coherence where there is none',[6] has dissuaded him from satisfying the demands of an audience that presumably craves the artificial structure and order that a story seems to promise with a traditional filmic narrative. Similarly, the suggestion that stories tend to create connections where there are none, particularly where the filmic/photographic image does not suggest any such connections, has made Wenders wary of traditional filmic narrative.

The other side to Wenders' considerations regards the image. He quotes the film theoretician Béla Balázs in response to the existential question put to him in a questionnaire – 'Why do you make films?':

> [Balázs] talks about the ability (and the responsibility) of cinema 'to show things as they are'. And he says cinema can 'rescue the existence of things'. That's precisely it.[7]

This is a purely phenomenological idea of cinema based on three points: the act of showing something; the act of retaining an image of that thing's physical appearance; and the responsibility to do this in a spirit of sincerity, to show things 'as they are.' Elsewhere, Wenders refers to the Lumière brothers' *L'arriveé d'un train en gare* (1895) as 'a moment of truth'.[8] While he sites the act of recording an image of physical reality as the original role of cinema here, he also implies, through his choice of words, that this act has been a source of cinematic creativity, and that the physical act of seeing again, or of recognising a given reality in the recorded image, can be a poetic experience:

> Around seventy years ago someone set up a camera for the very first time to capture movement in eighteen pictures per second, so that later on he could recognise on the screen what he had already seen through the lens: how someone turns his head, how clouds move across the sky, how grass trembles, how a face shows pain or joy.[9]

From Wenders' words, we can speculate that the act of recording the visible world for others to view at a later time constitutes a creative act in itself, and that this creative act has moral responsibilities attached to it. Not the act of recording but the truthfulness of a photographic representation is a moral duty in this sense, precisely because such photographic representations (today one must include the electronic image-making technologies under the term 'photographic') are able to provide the truest available image of the physical appearance of things for the world to see.

The moral aspect of Wenders' aesthetic also rests on the recognition that images today permeate all aspects of everyday life, and that they are a standard by which, like a look into the mirror, identity is formed and fixed. Writing on *The State of Things* (1982), the German film critic Frieda Grafe explains the importance of this function of images in the following terms:

Anyone who complains that there is too much talk about film-making [in *The State of Things*] ... should consider that it is vitally important for us to know more about the origins of images. Because they make us more than ever.[10]

For such a mirror to be useful in the process of determining identity, the reflection in the mirror must be true. The decisive powers that Wenders attributes to film images in the identification processes of human beings lies in their 'photographic' nature. Considering his references to Balázs in *The Logic of Images*, Wenders believes that those who generate images – the film-makers – have a responsibility to guarantee their authenticity: the affirmation and preservation of the integrity of images. Accordingly, the photographic image, the technical basis of cinema, becomes one of the main themes in Wenders' work.

The tendency, as he describes it, for a story to falsify or pervert the truth latently contained within photographic and film images by creating connections that may not exist in the corresponding reality, is a threat to the integrity of the image. This tension is at the centre of the reflexive debate on image and narrative in Wenders' work and writings, namely the declared aim of finding a balance that simultaneously grants the spectator a story without allowing the story to determine or influence the meaning of a film's images, and that provides a framework structure for the presentation of his images.

Critical analyses of Wenders' films typically praise their images with grandiose terms such as 'a feast for the eye'[11] but express consternation at the lacking coherence of their narratives. Writing on *Far Away, So Close*, Frank Schnelle perhaps best exhibits the tendency to expect a traditional narrative structure in cinema, considering the combination of a strong emphasis on the image with the refusal to wrap up events into a less than challenging story an unqualified cinematic failure:

The great paradox in this film: on one hand Wenders seems to be doing everything in his power to resist telling anything like a story. On the other hand, he weaves a multitude of destinies and episodes into a monstrosity of a story [...] Wenders films against film; he is a classic example of the man who saws off the very branch he is sitting on. This time he has fallen off the branch – presumably for good.[12]

The ways in which Wenders has consistently sought methods of coping with, indeed promoting, the idea of cinema as a medium capable of incorporating forms of narrative without himself falling back on established narrative traditions in his work, and how he attempts to guard the integrity of the image against manipulation through narrative influences, provides a valuable insight into the relevance of his work for cinema on the whole. And if Wenders can say at one and the same time that 'I totally reject stories'[13] but also that he does, in fact, try to tell stories,[14] what kind of stories are these?

This book will explore some of the elementary theoretical positions that inform or are of primary relevance to Wenders' film aesthetic. Chapter One focuses on the particularly intimate relationship the filmic image has with reality, by virtue of its photographic nature, but also on the conflicts that emerge from the assertion that this reality is in fact illusory, existing, as it does, only in the films' images. Chapter Two takes on the filmic narrative, first in the context of Wenders' belief in the incompatibility of images and stories, and then moving to an analysis of the narrative structure of the tales that Wenders does, despite his mistrust of stories, tell in his films. As both these first chapters are heavily theory-oriented, Chapter Three closely analyses a representative selection of six of Wenders' films with the aim of addressing the problematic described above, and covering in depth Wenders' career from the first to the very latest independent feature films, including one of the meditative documentary films for which Wenders is well-known. But first, a little background information.

Wenders and the New German Cinema

Wenders' concentration on the metalinguistic analysis of the filmic medium has remained the most dominant and relevant thematic tendency in his oeuvre. This is one of many stylistic and thematic aspects of his work that distinguishes him from his colleagues within the categorising body of the New German Cinema, but in this respect the director with whom one might most closely identify Wenders is Edgar Reitz. Like Wenders, Reitz attempts a redemption of the cinema in the face of its decline with his concept of *Kino Utopia*. The main difference between their positions is, however, that Reitz aims for a radical restructuring of film and cinema itself – cinema architecture, projection conventions, film form, content and structure – whereas Wenders concentrates reflexively on the aesthetics of the essential elements that make up film: its sound, its images, the stories that it tells and how they all combine. [15]

Werner Herzog would, in contrast, seem to be on a similar search for pure and transparent images as Wenders, 'a space for human honour and respect, landscapes not yet offended, planets that don't exist yet, dreamed landscapes'.[16] But whereas Wenders seeks out his images in the cities, amongst the people or on the roads that link the cities, Herzog dreams of outer-space, the depths of the South American or African jungle or the deserts of Australia, far removed from the places where human life is to be found. This is a luxury that Wenders frequently allows himself, but never for more than a fleeting and escapist view of the wing of a jet flying high above the clouds, or in the dreams of one of his lonely heroes.

In contrast to Herzog's starkly metaphysical view of reality, Rainer Werner Fassbinder approaches socio-political issues directly, in a way that is almost completely alien to Wenders, though they do share many stylistic traits. Fassbinder's career parallels that of Wenders in their shared early experimentation with unconventional forms and in their later common activity of synthesising mostly American genre forms. Both approached traditional American genres, according to Thomas Elsaesser, because of the different 'attitude' towards the characters: 'Via genre films, West German directors became sensitive towards a new sense of realism which had to do not only with a different attitude to the protagonist, but also with a different approach to time in the cinema. This applies especially to Wim Wenders.'[17] For Wenders, the main American cinematic influences were undoubtedly the western and the road movie genres, whereas Fassbinder had a particularly high regard for the German émigré director Douglas Sirk, whose melodramas were, similarly, often about losers on the edge of society. Fassbinder's heroes are, instead, those who failed to make use of the material benefits of post-war Germany.[18] Stylistically, Fassbinder's formal beauty, his expressive use of colour, lighting and decor are far removed from Wenders' refusal to manipulate colour and light and his often forlornly desolate scenes. References to the German past are often more obliquely stated in Wenders than in Fassbinder and, until 1987, there are only a few specific allusions to the past.

Finally, though, Wenders must be considered, just as his great inspiration Nicholas Ray was in Hollywood, more an outsider to the New German Cinema than an insider. In a process that often seems more like identification with outside influences such as the American western, Wenders has consistently referred either to the German past, more accurately the pre-Second World War German cinema, in search of his idols, or he has looked away from his country. Whilst many of his contemporary colleagues turned their attention during the 1970s and 1980s to the problems of terrorism, feminist and political issues, or the continuing issue of coming to terms with the then-recent German past in films such as *Germany in Autumn* (Alexander Kluge *et al.* 1978), *The Patriot* (Alexander Kluge, 1979), *The German Sisters/The Leaden Times* (Margarethe von Trotta, 1981), *Germany, Pale Mother* (Helma Sanders-Brahms, 1980), *The Marriage of Maria Braun* and *The Third Generation* (Rainer Werner Fassbinder, 1979), *Hitler: A Film from Germany* (Hans Jürgen Syberberg, 1979), and *Knife in the Head* (Reinhard Hauff,

1978), Wenders' main concern was with what happened in the cinema during and after the Nazi period and the implications of this for the cinema of today. The first time he directly approaches feminist issues – and in this respect, as a man, he is one of only a few to do so – was with the film *Paris, Texas* (1984), but even this example focuses, in the end, more on the image of women in cinema and in advertising.

Wenders' written commentaries on two films, Joachim C. Fest and Christian Herrendoerfer's *Hitler: A Career* (1976/77) and Peter Fonda and Dennis Hopper's *Easy Rider* (1969), illustrate his view that his identification with the nascent German cinema movement extends little further than co-operation after the many years that the German cinema had been out in the cold. His article *That's entertainment: Hitler*[19] places emphasises on the degradation he perceives the German film industry to have suffered through the Nazi period, claiming that this resulted in the loss of a native film tradition with which the post-war generation of German film-makers and the New German Cinema, led by Alexander Kluge, could identify:

> And I speak for everyone who, over the last few years, after a long, barren period, has started producing sounds and images again, in a country that has a profound mistrust of sounds and images about itself, that has therefore, over the last thirty years, greedily swallowed up all the foreign images it could, as long as they distracted it from itself. I don't think that any other country has had such a loss of faith in its own images, stories and myths as we have. We, the directors of the New Cinema, have felt this loss most keenly: in ourselves as the absence of a tradition of our own, as a generation without fathers; and in our audiences as confusion and apprehension.[20]

Here, Wenders considers a very human reality in post-war Germany, but rather than analysing the loss he perceives the German people to have suffered as a symptom of that past, he considers it in cinematic terms: how will the cinema cope? Though he claims to speak for everyone, he draws a line between himself and those of his colleagues who take a more direct approach to confronting the past, while at the same time distancing himself from that past, attempting to mediate through the filter of a cinematic context.

Similarly, Wenders' point of view differs significantly from that of most of his colleagues on the question of politics in film: whilst never having believed that overtly political films are a realistic way of achieving goals (curiously, this was Hitler's very tactic), Wenders considers every film to be political: 'Most political of all are those that pretend not to be: "entertainment" movies.'[21] Here, Wenders is mostly attacking the idea that films should tell anything at all, himself favouring the path of showing. Speaking of his own film *The American Friend* (1977), he states that it is:

> … 'entertainment', and it's exciting. But it doesn't affirm the status quo. On the contrary: everything is fluid, open, under threat. The film has no explicit political content. But it doesn't talk down to you. It doesn't treat its characters like marionettes – nor its audience either. A lot of 'political' films, unfortunately, do.[22]

Easy Rider, in contrast…

> … isn't a political film just because it shows Peter Fonda and Dennis Hopper dealing in cocaine at the beginning, or because it shows them getting thrown in jail for nothing, being simply shot down, or because it shows Jack Nicholson being shot by vigilantes, or how a sheriff is allowed to behave. It is political because it is beautiful: because the country that the two huge motor-bikes drive through is beautiful; because the images that the film gives of this country are beautiful and peaceful; because the music you hear in the film is beautiful; because Peter Fonda moves in a beautiful way; because you can see that Dennis Hopper is not only acting, but that he is also in the process of making a film.[23]

Wenders' concept of what makes films political – particularly American films – thus seems to differ from the apparent norms of the New German Cinema in that he believes a film that seeks to avoid controversy has the presumably intentional effect of implying that the state of affairs is satisfactory. This is borne out by David A. Cook's assertion that:

> Everything that characterised Hollywood between 1952 and 1965 can be understood as a response to anti-Communist hysteria and the blacklist on one hand, and to the advent of television … on the other. In the name of combating Communism, films of serious social comment … could no longer be made. Instead, westerns, musical comedies, lengthy costume epics and other traditional genre fare – sanitised and shorn of political content – became the order of the day.[24]

Such examples as these show that in a time when the New German Cinema was making a name for itself internationally, succeeding in the process of self-definition during the late 1970s and early 1980s, Wenders' central ideological and political positions, and his view of the recent German past, differed from the norm in the sense that they were *film*-ideological, *film*-political and *film*-historical positions. Or, as Norbert Grob puts it, Wenders was more interested in making films *politically* than in making *political* films, and it is this that led Elsaesser to identify Wenders' commentary on Rudolf Thome's *Red Sun* (1969) – praising its simplicity and its narrative, one that does not impose itself on the characters – as a direct attack on the 'moral and ideological buttonholing' of the New German Cinema, and thus a 'condemnation of Kluge'.[25]

Wenders' initial sources of cinematic inspiration and identification, then, lay elsewhere, namely in the traditional American western of the 1940s and 1950s, and in pre-war German cinema. In his essay *The American Dream*, Wenders points to the influence of the American cinema in his early years: 'But it was always obvious just what their American language was: a different sense of life.'[26] And: 'I vaguely knew that, unlike in Germany, there was nothing to hide there.'[27]

These influences appear in many different forms in Wenders' cinema, from the characters and narratives that recall the films and the person of Nicholas Ray, to whom Wenders pays homage in *Nick's Film: Lightning Over Water* (1980), innumerable references to Ray and John Ford in films like *Alice in the Cities* (1974) and *Kings of the Road* (1976), the use of pin-ball machines, juke-boxes, comic-strips, and soundtracks usually made up of American, but sometimes British, rock music. Robert Phillip Kolker and Peter Beicken make particular reference to the figure of Ethan Edwards from John Ford's film *The Searchers* (1956) who, they say, permeates all of Wenders' films including *Kings of the Road* and *Paris, Texas*.[28] Wenders himself sees the major achievement of classical American cinema as

> the collective narrative that came out of the studio system. All the myths that related the cinema to the great narratives in other media were created by this collective narration. Neither the European film nor the 'auteur' movie ever managed that. None of us has been able to tell stories like that. Our stories were all subjective.[29]

Objective stories, 'a different sense of life', and 'having nothing to hide', then, are the qualities that Wenders appreciated in American cinema, and that drew him away from identification with his contemporaries at home. Although Kolker and Beicken would have it that Ford was above all a visual influence on Wenders,[30] the same was true of his stories, such as the classical Fordian themes of travel, or the turmoil of the individual in an alien environment and in situations of extreme stress as in *The Searchers* (1956) or *Stagecoach* (1939). Almost all of Wenders' central characters travel, and their journeys through the world are often the only thing that keeps the narrative flowing. Similarly, the situations they encounter on their journeys are often laden with tension, for example the fight between Robert and Bruno that ends the journey in *Kings of the Road* and functions as a release from the tension that builds up during their progress along the former East-West German border in a truck. Visually, it is beyond doubt that Wenders was impressed by Ford's wide-open, stylised landscapes and elaborate tracking shots: time and again, Ford filmed in Monument Valley in the south-west of the USA, a location to which Wenders himself came for the opening sequences of *Paris, Texas.*

In Ford it was the constant slow movement of the narrative and visual simplicity that attracted Wenders, but he considered Nicholas Ray, an outsider in Hollywood, to be a truly pioneering director: 'Ray *did* invent the cinema. Not many do.'[31] Here, Wenders refers to a particular scene from Ray's film *The Lusty Men* (1951), which he 'stole' for his own *Kings of the Road*. He praises the flow of Ray's story, how it advances without any pressure or sense of haste. The scene in which the main protagonist, played by Robert Mitchum, goes back to the house where he was born and takes out a dusty box in which he had left a few coins and a revolver says more to Wenders about homecoming than any other.[32]

These, then, were the objective stories that Wenders values in pre-1950s American cinema. They offered him 'a different sense of life' to that experienced in Germany during the immediate post-war years; the images of the wide expanse of the American south-west, where there was 'nothing to hide'. The most important formative cinematic influence on Wenders was thus an illusionist-realist cinema, steeped in the myths of the past of a nation that was culturally colonising the world, creating new myths that corresponded to the dreams of the film-maker's generation.

But there was another history closer to home that could not simply be transcended through the new, surrogate American culture. The influence of Ford and Ray's films on Wenders was, to a certain extent, a response to the perceived cultural vacuum in Germany after the Second World War, but they also seemed to endorse Wenders' adoption, as a cinematic father, of the exiled German director Fritz Lang in the face of his persecution in Germany as a deserter or suspected fascist collaborator. Lang fled to the US before the war began and only returned to Germany when the war was over, where he was coolly received. Wenders, in contrast, looked to Lang as one of the lost fathers of German cinema, and so it comes as no surprise that in the same film in which he pays tribute to Ray, the 'inventor of cinema', he also pays tribute to Lang in the year of his death, 1976. The two directors are firmly linked in *Kings of the Road* via the theme of mourning: mourning Lang's death and, through the association with Ray via the quotation of the Mitchum scene in *The Lusty Men*, mourning Lang – as much as Ray an outsider – as the personification of the lost home and tradition of the German cinema. In his article on Lang, *Death is no Solution*, Wenders expresses his anger at how he was someone who was

> getting noticed because he was dead who hadn't been noticed when he was alive. The obituaries on television and in the newspapers didn't seem to me to be quite right. I couldn't get rid of the feeling that they showed a sense of relief, or the reverse, of unease. And the thoroughly proper lines about Lang's importance in the development of the cinema and its language sounded almost like excuses. Now he's dead they want to turn him into a myth as soon as possible. Crap. His death is no solution.[33]

Perhaps this is why, in 1980, Wenders filmicly documented the last days of Nicholas Ray in the film *Nick's Film: Lightning Over Water*. Again, Wenders *film*-historically objectifies the past.

Besides the American directors, there are two other figures who have significantly influenced Wenders' work, but in different ways: the Italian director Michelangelo Antonioni and the Japanese director Yasujiro Ozu. It was on Antonioni's prompting at the Cannes Film Festival in 1982 that Wenders first began to experiment with video technology, a change of heart which has become the rule rather than the exception in almost all of his films since then.[34] In addition to this, some of the most explicitly 'borrowed' scenes in Wenders' oeuvre are direct quotations from Antonioni's films: the colour green in *The American Friend* from *Blow Up* (1966), and the desert flight in a light aircraft in *Until the End of the World* (1991) from *Zabriskie Point* (1969). Antonioni is also the only other director with whom Wenders has collaborated in the direction of a film since his film-school years: *Beyond the Clouds* (1995).

As with Ray, Wenders dedicated a film to Ozu, entitled *Tokyo Ga* (1985), in which Wenders describes his admiration for Ozu in the following terms:

> If our century still had any shrines ... if there were any relics of the cinema, then for me it would have to be the corpus of the Japanese director Yazujiro Ozu [...] Ozu's films always tell the same simple stories, of the same people, in

the same city of Tokyo. They are told with extreme economy, reduced to their bare essentials.[35]

It was primarily his narrative style and his method of building his characters through their interaction with a landscape that attracted Wenders to Ozu. In 1976 he admitted having understood that it was 'right to refuse to explain things, that it is possible to explain them better by showing them ... That's just why Ozu is the only director I have learned from. His way of telling stories was, in the most absolute sense, representational.'[36] Despite the two filmic diaries he made in Japan, *Tokyo Ga* and *Notes on Cities and Clothes* (1989), which both research Japanese life in Tokyo, this culture does not seem to have influenced his work either formally or thematically to the same extent as American culture, which informs every film he has made. Wenders' interest seems to have remained restricted to Ozu the film-maker, whose culture fascinates Wenders but is, finally, perhaps too alien to allow close identification. In both Ozu and the American directors, Wenders appreciated above all the simplicity of image and story, the calmness of the films and their narrative continuity.

Central themes

After the completion of his first films for television, *The Goalkeeper's Fear of the Penalty Kick* (1971) and *The Scarlet Letter* (1972), Wenders began *Alice in the Cities* in the USA in 1973. Critics agree that this film was the first manifestation of Wenders' style, and Wenders himself claims to have found his individual voice in cinema with it.[37] The film begins with a fairly standard narrative about a man who, before returning to Europe having failed to complete a task allocated to him, by chance meets a mother and child and is forced, with the disappearance of the mother, to accompany the child on her return journey to Europe. The story then takes on the form of a more liberal, unplanned and episodic narrative as the pair search for a house once occupied by the child's grandmother in the German Ruhr region. The film continues the theme of observation of the outside world already apparent in Wenders' school films, but emphasises the problems of vision and perception in the modern world, contrasting a vision mediated through television, photography and cinema with the mechanicalness of a child's habitual perception, as Wenders seeks to recuperate a pure vision through and in cinema. The protagonist, Philip Winter (Rüdiger Vogler), bemoans the monotonous American television and radio programmes, the hotels that are the same everywhere, and that these conditions threaten to estrange one from oneself. The chance meeting with the child, Alice (Yella Rottländer) provides Winter with a story to follow and a new, childlike vision that offers him the possibility of regaining his lost subjectivity. Like most of its predecessors, *Alice in the Cities* is also a road movie – a genre with which the author was to become synonymous – that documents the movement of a figure through the USA, then, together with the young Alice, through the Netherlands and the German Ruhr.

Kings of the Road is another such road movie, but this time the journey follows a route along the East German/West German border from one provincial town to the next. Like *Alice in the Cities*, it features high-contrast black and white film-stock and a slow narrative movement, leading the Italian critic Filippo D'Angelo to describe it as 'almost a documentary'.[38] Here, more than in any previous film, Wenders makes use of the landscape through which his characters pass to find the story for the film. This may perhaps lie chiefly in the fact that after the first week's rushes were useless due to a fault in the film-stock, Wenders had little more than a road-map marking all the rural cinema towns along the border to work with, and few ideas. The result was that he would write a rough script in the evening, often through the night before shooting, and had little idea of what the next day would bring until he had seen the location. This loose story follows the characters, who follow the lines on Wenders' road-map. The story was 'found' on location.

Story remains loosely structured and relatively subordinated to the image in all of Wenders' films until 1977 when he filmed the Patricia Highsmith novel, *Ripley's Game*. Calling the film *The American Friend*, Wenders adopts and adapts the traditional American gangster genre, already a feature in early films such as *Same Player Shoots Again* (1967), *Alabama: 2000 Light Years from Home* (1968), and *Summer in the City (Dedicated to The Kinks)* (1970). All the gangsters are played by famous directors or figures in the film industry, 'because they're the only rascals I know, and the only ones who make life and death decisions as airily as the Mafia'.[39] The story takes on stronger features than the previous films, due to the use of a published novel. But, in accordance with the conventions of the genre, the criminal element in *The American Friend,* and especially the character of Ripley (Dennis Hopper), are based on the cinematic codes of the genre, and are thus more strongly characterised than in any of the earlier films. This is also the first film in which Wenders makes significant expressive use of colour since *Same Player Shoots Again*.

Wenders had long toyed with the idea of working in an American environment until, finally, Francis Ford Coppola invited him to direct a film he was producing: *Hammett* (1982). Wenders himself has all but disowned this film, over which he felt he had no control, and the most interesting results of this experiment were the reactions to his experiences in Hollywood and his film *The State of Things* (1982). Here, Wenders first seems to begrudgingly admit that stories are a necessity in cinema. The film reflects filmic narration at its roots as Wenders continues the theme of cinema as commerce touched on in *The American Friend*. Two ideas of cinema are placed in opposition to one another: European cinema and Hollywood, where story is dominant and black and white is reduced to a form for small, 'serious' films. Friedrich Munro (Patrick Bachau), the main protagonist of *The State of Things*, believes in the power of the image to tell the story, but as he is financed by shady creditors in Los Angeles who demand a colour film with a story to ensure a profit is made, he is inevitably drawn into a story himself, which ends in his death and the death of his European artistic ideals. Although Wenders is cautious on the matter, Munro should absolutely be identified with his creator, who, after the turbulent experience of Hollywood, was experiencing a similar crisis of cinematic identity, on one hand trying to affirm his identity as a European film-maker, while being forced to give up his ideals, his faith in images, by an industry that considers a film without a story like 'a house without walls'.[40]

If *The State of Things* attempted to review Wenders' position claiming the image as the sole guardian of film as art, then *Paris, Texas* examines the power of images to degrade. So far, women had remained largely on the periphery of the diegesis, but here, Wenders uses the advertising industry as an example to illustrate how, through its images, the public image of women has suffered, become one-dimensional, fulfilling only a commercial function. Film here acts as a kind of memory through which redemption is promised. The final sequence of the film is one of the most important, but also one of the most often misinterpreted sequences in Wenders' work to date, and represents Wenders' confession of having contributed to this state of affairs. *Paris, Texas* is a visually stunning film with an equally rich soundtrack but, following the defeat of *The State of Things,* it also relies on more ordinary composition, dialogue and cutting-patterns and, possibly as a result of Wenders' collaboration with the script-writer Sam Shepard, has a more conventional narrative structure. Nevertheless, the film remains open, a constant sign of opposition in Wenders to the conventions of dominant – American – narrative cinema, as the film's title suggests. Also, for the first time in Wenders' work, this film gives an initial clue that narrative of a kind may provide the answer to the crisis in his personal film aesthetic, evidenced in *The State of Things*: having begun with wide images of the American south-west and a seemingly dumb central character, *Paris, Texas* comes to a close in a verbal avalanche in which a story is related.

More self-assured in dealing with story after the success of *Paris, Texas*, Wenders makes this the subject of his next feature, *Wings of Desire* (1987). Drawing on Walter Benjamin's concept of time and history, Wenders brings this idea down to an everyday level to build a coherent story out of the individual fragments of ordinary peoples' lives. He raises the status of cinema and its capability of combining word with image into a new myth-making narrative that can give the world an image of itself. Already in the early days, Wenders exhibited a tendency for the observation of small, ordinary details, but only now does he confirm this activity filmicly, as a concept of great general importance to the world. Significantly, also, it is a woman, Marion (Solveig Dommartin), who gathers up the fragments of her life to turn them into a story. Equipped with the now usual combination of Jürgen Knieper's music and a rock 'n' roll soundtrack, *Wings of Desire* represents a new step in Wenders' experimentation with film sound: 'I've never done anything where the sound alone is like a whole film itself ... Where there's so much to hear simultaneously, because so much is told simultaneously.'[41]

Wenders' longest and most ambitious project to date, *Until the End of the World*, was first planned while he was in Australia in 1977. Understandably, therefore, this film embraces many of the topics that preoccupied the director during this fourteen year period. In the film, he projects a futuristic image of the world at the end of the twentieth century, a world in which digital video and computer-generated images have a controlling force in people's lives. Wenders takes this notion to the extreme, imagining a world in which video can lead to psychic illness, similar to a narcotic addiction. The cure for the illness of images, Wenders suggests, is to be found in more archaic art forms – painting and the written and spoken word. As in the two previous features, it is again a woman who takes control of events, and who has the vision to determine the development of the narrative. With a stronger story in this film, Wenders appears to come closer to overcoming his doubts about narrative.

Taken by surprise by the fall of the Berlin Wall in 1989, Wenders returned to the city in 1993 to make *Far Away, So Close*, an unplanned sequel to *Wings of Desire*. Time is the main theme in this movie, with one of the fallen angels being dragged into a story that develops too quickly for him to cope with, driving him and the story to a sudden and tragic death. The film was not well received by critics, and represents the beginning of a period in which many, including Wenders himself, began to wonder about his future as a director. Other films produced in this nevertheless extremely productive period were *Lisbon Story* (1994), *Beyond the Clouds* (1995, together with Michelangelo Antonioni), *A Trick of the Light* (1996), and *The End of Violence* (1997).

As if testing his conviction that music had saved his life once before,[42] Wenders took advantage of Ry Cooder's rediscovery and reinvigoration of Cuban music in 1999 to make the digitally-shot film *Buena Vista Social Club* (1999), which became one of the most successful documentary films ever. His latest feature project, *The Million*

Dollar Hotel (1999), also has a strong musical basis: co-written and co-produced by U2 singer Bono, the film continues Wenders' discourse on the commercialisation of images.

Wenders' latest documentary on the German rock band BAP, entitled *Ode to Cologne: A Rock 'n' Roll Film*, was premiered at the Berlin Festival in February 2002. He also premiered a ten-minute short at the Cannes Festival in May 2002 entitled *Twelve Miles to Trona* as part of a compliation on the theme of time called *Ten Minutes Older*, involving directors such as Aki Kaurismäki, Werner Herzog, Jim Jarmusch and Spike Lee. Wenders is currently working on two projects: a documentary on the history of Blues music (in association with Martin Scorsese) and a road movie set in the USA, a further collaboration with scriptwriter Sam Sheperd.

CHAPTER ONE

on the production of images

The seventh art, as it is called, is able to get to the essence of things, to capture the climate and the currents of their time, to express the hopes and the fears and the desires as a popular mass language like nothing else.[1]

The camera never lies: image and reality

The circumstance that allows physical reality to appear in film or in a photograph just as it appears when viewed without the mediation of a camera or other optical device – meaning that the physiognomy of things can be reproduced exactly, but in two dimensions – has encouraged the acceptance in everyday life of photographic evidence as indisputably authentic. This is true even if most people are aware that photographs are easily manipulated to show a reality or an event that never in fact existed or took place. The ability of cinema to produce an accurate image of physical reality means that the claim of truth is always latently possible. People therefore customarily believe that what they see in a photograph, or almost any kind of photographic image, is genuine. The English language has even gained a new phrase since the invention of photography to reflect this: the camera never lies.

The film camera itself is a neutral piece of apparatus that enables the production of images with varying degrees of digression from the original. Robert Bresson expresses the camera's neutrality in relation to other recording devices in the following way, drawing attention also to the fact that any particular intent in the image-making process lies with the user of the cinematic apparatus, rather than with the apparatus itself:

> What the human eye, the pencil, brush or quill cannot hope to capture, the camera catches without even knowing what it is, and holds onto it with the assured indifference of a machine.[2]

Where distortion or any other disfigurement of physical reality occurs in the image – in telephoto or wide-angle shots particularly – efforts are generally made to reduce this to a minimum unless the effect is intentional. For Edgar Morin, photographic images leave the impression of being real themselves through their analogy to the contours of the real object, even though the ability to convince of a photographic image is compromised by abstracting aspects such as their two-dimensionality or, sometimes, black and white images. At the same time, he identifies the rendering of movement in the film image – a condition made possible by film's temporal dimension – as an aspect of film that can increase the impression of plausibility:

> The film unfolds and continues. At the same time, the objects put in motion fill the space ... The connection between the reality of the movement and the appearance of the forms produces a feeling of concrete life and an experience of objective reality. The forms lend the motion an objective framework, and the framework lends the forms a bodily mass.[3]

As a film-maker concerned with the documentation of the time in which he lives,[4] Wenders has made the photographic/filmic image the basis of his cinema, in which the relationship between image and reality is central to his film-aesthetic. From the title of Wenders' first film, *Schauplätze* (*Locations*, 1967)[5] it would seem that the interest in observation of the environment has occupied the director since his beginnings. Several fragments of this film have been retained and incorporated into *Same Player Shoots Again*, which exhibits an observing tendency that one might have expected from *Schauplätze*, and that remained common to later films. These early films showed the euphoria of someone using the medium for the first time, but not yet able to master its codes and instead being dragged along by its 'magical' reproductive abilities. This includes a respect for objects and phenomena, and for real spatial and temporal dimensions, evidenced through the almost exclusive use of long, uninterrupted shots, a static camera and a refusal to use editing for synthetic or dramatic effects. Many scenes, shots and sequences are taken from a window of a building or of a moving car, leading Grob to describe these films as a 'look out of a window'.[6]

In emphasising the particular ability of film and photography to accurately record the appearance of physical reality, Wenders takes up not only the position of Balázs on the relationship between cinema and reality, but also allies himself with Siegfried Kracauer's film theory. Central to Kracauer's theory is the fundamental role that photography plays in film: '[Photography] is and remains the decisive factor in establishing film content. The nature of photography survives in that of film.'[7] More precisely, it is the optical conditions that allow for the exact reproduction of physical reality that Kracauer considers decisive for the aesthetics of film production.

> Like photography, film tends to cover all material phenomena virtually within reach of the camera. To express the same otherwise, it is as if the medium were animated by the chimerical desire to establish the continuum of physical existence.[8]

Pier Paolo Pasolini, however, takes the relation film has with reality to its most extreme and radical end. In his book *Empirismo eretico* Pasolini brings the cinema and the world together as one, labelling reality as '*kino in natura*'.[9] This conception describes reality as cinema but without a camera, and cinema as reality, but reproduced by an invisible camera in an unbroken continuity.

> This *kino in natura*, which is reality, actually represents a language that resembles our oral speech in certain ways. Cinema is – because it reproduces reality – reality's written aspect ... it represents reality through reality ... This philosophy seems to me to be nothing else than a blind, childish and pragmatic liking for reality. As endless and continuous [as] reality may be, an ideal camera can always reproduce it in its endlessness and continuity. Cinema is, in the first and archetypal sense of the term, a continuous and endless series of shots.[10]

Film images are thus not to be considered symbolic, according to Pasolini, because they represent reality with reality. The reproductive ability of the filmic medium implies that cinema has, above all, a documentary role to play in the field of artistic creativity.

Wenders makes the image the basis of his cinema, which we might with good reason call a documentary cinema, because the cinema-image is ideally suited to the documentation of the visual world, the illusion of actual presence. Entertainment, comedy, thrillers – all these other functions that film has assumed since its invention – do not depend on the existence of film or photography, whereas the documentation of the appearance of things does. Of the other visual arts, painting is the nearest, but, although theoretically possible, it does not naturally fit into the role of copying the material world. In photography, it is difficult to avoid things appearing in the image just as they do in reality, even if the photograph is an abstraction.

For Wenders' cinema, the result of this choice of emphasis is that he tries to allow his films to remain open to material phenomena of both a specific and a non-specific nature; his films strive to emphasise the incorporation of the physical environments in which they play, including those films that follow their characters over sometimes vast distances around the world. For Wenders, realism is a code of representation, a *mise-en-scène* of objects and events that had not been visible before, or had not been thought worth preserving. This is what Wenders considers to have been the charm and aesthetic drive behind early cinema.

Rescuing physical reality

Combined with photography's ability to reproduce physical reality accurately and in a pictorial form that is easily accessed and processed by any viewer, the fact that a photographic image withstands the flow of time means that moments in time, and the physical appearance of objects, whether animate or inanimate, whether fleeting or permanent, can be preserved. Balázs spoke of a cinema capable of rescuing the existence of things, while Kracauer's *Theory of Film* is subtitled *The Redemption of Physical Reality*. Wenders understands the term 'redemption' to mean not just the preservation of the appearance of things, beings and moments in time, but more specifically the preservation of their identity:

> No other medium can treat the question of identity as searchingly or with as much justification as film. No other language is as capable of addressing itself to the physical reality of things. 'The possibility and the purpose of film is to show everything the way it is'. However exalted that sentence of Béla Balázs sounds, it's true. Reading it makes me want to see a film.[11]

As well as quoting Balázs when asked the question 'Why do you make films?', Wenders also found a phrase by Paul Cézanne important enough to remember: 'Things are disappearing. If you want to see anything, you have to hurry.'[12] For Wenders, the act of filming is 'a heroic act (not always, not often, but sometimes)'.[13] It enables the redemption of transient things as well as reproducing these accurately. Photography is perhaps the nearest mankind has ever come to achieving immortality for these two reasons. Of relevance in this respect is that photographic images can be retained almost indefinitely as proof of existence or of moments that become a part of the past immediately after they occur. Wenders explains this in simple terms:

> Something happens, you see it happening, you film it as it happens, the camera sees it and records it, and you can look at it again, afterwards. The thing itself may no longer be there, but you can still see it, the fact of its existence hasn't been lost ... The camera is a weapon against the tragedy of things, against their disappearing. Why make films? Bloody stupid question![14]

For Wenders, film becomes a tool capable of fixing and retaining identity through its ability to present an accurate picture of physical existence and to freeze transient appearance. Just as truth is latently possible in a photograph because it can provide an accurate reproduction of physical reality – proof of the existence of an object, or of a moment in time – a photograph is also a record that is valid even when the subject of the photograph no longer exists. The profusion in his films of images that document things, in particular, buildings that are about to disappear, suggests that there is a conscious effort on the part of the director to make use of cinema's ability to hold onto the appearance of things, preserving them until well after the objects themselves are forgotten. The house in which Jonathan, the main protagonist of *The American Friend*, lives is earmarked for demolition by the Hamburg Senate, and a demolition is under way in a scene in Paris; the cinema in *The Goalkeeper's Fear of the Penalty Kick* was reconstructed in a famous Jugendstil house due for destruction ('For the same reason, we used Wittgenstein's house in one of the scenes');[15] the Berlin Wall in *Wings of Desire* disappeared in 1989, prompting a discussion on whether it should not remain in part to preserve the memory of division. Wenders uses the ability of the photographic image to document not just the existence of things that are about to disappear, but to highlight the fleeting nature of physical existence. This characteristic of cinema prompted Jean Cocteau to describe the activity of filming as watching 'death at work'.[16]

Peter Buchka describes this notion, in connection with a memory from Wenders' days at film-school in Munich, as '*Zeitgeist*', or 'spirit of the age'.[17] He refers to an occasion, recounted by Wenders, when he was sitting in a Munich bar together with his colleague Rainer Werner Fassbinder; a woman (Hanna Schygulla) would regularly put a coin into a jukebox and dance alone in front of it. The two film-makers agreed that that was a scene worth filming, which Fassbinder did in his film *Die Ehe der Maria Braun* (*The Marriage of Maria Braun,* 1979). Buchka contests that, regardless of the fact that Schygulla went on to become a star of the German screen, or that meaning might have grown to the image with her rise to fame, the images would have represented a worthwhile record of a particular phenomenon:

> In this way, and above all, a fundamental respect for the simple appearance of a phenomenon – whether it is a person or whether it is an object – is expressed. And this appearance has a value of its own, regardless of which meaning history – or a story – may bestow upon it. This was the spirit of film right at the beginning. Lumière and his successors simply recorded what was of interest in their immediate vicinity: trains, horse-drawn carriages, people, things that moved.[18]

That constitutes, for Wenders, the particular ability of the cinema and the photographic image to record physical reality as something special precisely because the process of selecting such moments directs attention to them. In Wenders' cinema, the idea is to see the world as if for the first time, to try to catch hold of something that seems beautiful or interesting at the moment of its occurrence. Things are recorded just on their own merit, without needing to represent something else, they are there for themselves. Visual reality is itself a magical part of existence, but the cinema is capable of isolating things in a frame, making reality transparent, forcing the spectator to notice what they would otherwise have ignored.

In relation to his concept of cinema as the written language of reality, Pasolini speaks of film as performing a no less than revolutionary role in making reality transparent and promoting an awareness of physical existence:

> Just as written language has revolutionised spoken language, so too will cinema revolutionise reality. As long as the language of reality was a natural language, it lay beyond the limits of our consciousness; now, because we can see it in the cinema as a 'written' language, it necessarily demands a consciousness. The written language of reality above all has the effect that we recognise what the language of reality is; and, finally, that we change the way we think about reality.[19]

The film image as illusion of reality

Inherent to the filmic medium, the cinematic apparatus and to the act of image-viewing, however, is that no matter how much a director strives to remain faithful to the real appearance of physical reality, the aesthetic qualities of the medium dictate that any filmic or photographic image of a natural scene is always a reproduction of actuality in pictorial form. The term 'illusion' is more poignant because of the especially close resemblance film images can have to reality. In a sense, then, although Wenders might try to present an unmediated image of physical reality, the ideal of unmediated vision that he seems to have been suggesting in *Silver City* through the simulation of the blinking action remains unattainable: the film image remains an imitation of reality from the very start. Nevertheless, the accurate pictorial reproduction of physical reality represents an adequate goal in the work of Wim Wenders, while the limitations of the medium – the fact that depicted reality is never more than a reproduction – is thematically expressed as an inadequacy.[20]

Any portrayal of physical existence in a filmic or photographic representation is the product of mediation on various levels, each of which, according to André Bazin, increases the discrepancy between original and copy:

> The same event, the same object is subject to various different forms of representation. Each of these omits some characteristics, but preserves others, by which we are able to recognise the object on the screen. Each of them, for didactic or aesthetic purposes, effects an either higher or lower degree of abstraction, which prevents the original from appearing as a whole. At the end of this inevitable and necessary chemical process, the original source reality has been substituted by an illusion of reality.[21]

Although this characteristic of filmic and photographic images as, by definition, mere illusions of reality does not have any direct bearing on Wenders' desire for an unmediated representation of reality, the technical nature of the medium nevertheless makes such images the media most suited to enabling the realisation of this goal. The act of showing is therefore the first main instance of mediation between a direct view of reality and a portrayal of reality in images, and is a result of the spatial separation of film set from movie theatre. The point of view offered and the content of film images are exclusively the result of the director's choice. In this respect, the act of showing is, presumably, a compromise for Wenders because the medium is incapable of offering the audience its own point of view. A film-maker can do no more than to show what s/he sees, the way s/he sees it, and whether or not this amounts to an active deception of the audience (a moral question for Wenders) depends on how the material is presented.

The fact that film is a recording art also imposes a degree of temporal separation on events portrayed in film images, between the actual time of the occurrence of an event and the time the event is reviewed in a film. An event in reality is part of an infinite chain of concurrent and consecutive events, whether related or unrelated. The same event recorded on film is isolated from surrounding events by the necessity of turning on and off the film camera, which extracts an image of the event from the chain it organically belongs to and constructs a new context for it to appear in. Which events are recorded is again the choice of the director, as is the decision whether or not to place the recorded event into temporal relation with others. For Wenders, the necessity of making such decisions seemed, during the filming of *The Goalkeeper's Fear of the Penalty Kick*, to compromise the goal of unmediated representation:

> In every scene, my biggest problem is always how to end it and go on to the next one. Ideally I would show the time in between as well ... Every action – everything the goalkeeper does in our film, for instance – everything continues, and what you show is actually just a part of it. That's the hardest thing for me, how to choose what to show.[22]

The temporal and spatial aberrations that separate a portrayal of reality in the form of photographic images from the reality from which it is taken mean that cinema can provide no more than an illusion of reality. While Wenders has attempted in his early films to simulate the conditions of actual and contemporaneous observation, the fact that an illusion of reality is the closest the filmic medium can come to touching the surface of reality by no means excludes the ability of the medium to offer an accurate representation of physical existence. This is a characteristic inherent to the medium, but has relevance nevertheless, because the act of showing involves the use of such simulation. The very same attributes – temporal delay in the immediacy of a photographic representation of reality and spatial displacement of objects in images – are, in fact, necessary conditions for the act of showing. More importantly, these forms of mediation furnish the film-maker with the opportunity to mould what is to be shown into a personally constructed recreation of reality, employing various strategies and techniques that give cinema its aesthetic form, making it a creative art. They are the tools of intent in film, that would be denied to the film-maker if the film image were not an illusion of physical reality, and have relevance for filmic narration.

The inflation and reproduction of images

The act of showing involves the reproduction of reality in pictorial form which, in turn, requires the production of an illusion of reality. Ideally, Wenders would like to enable spectators of his films to enjoy unmediated visual perception, for his films to promote the act of seeing amongst his audience. The aesthetic and physical characteristics of cinema – his chosen art-form – dictate, however, that this sentiment can only be expressed through the mediation of photographic images, which are themselves reproductions of reality. Whilst considering the cinema an adequate tool for the promotion of visual perception, Wenders also feels that unrestricted and uncontrolled image-making can and has contributed to a deterioration in peoples' ability to understand their relation to and connection with what they see, and to a change in their seeing habits. Wenders' cinema is, at the time of *Alice in the Cities*, about the mediation between the human being and its environment, about the relationship between them and how this has changed since the invention – if one wished to take the theme back to its origins – of machines of mass-production: the printing-press, photography, the cinema itself. He relates how the process of conserving images, of holding up the disappearance of things was begun by poets and painters:

> At some time photography came along, and of course print existed already, and so you had the reproduction of painted images, that was the next step. Then film images, and now electronic images as well. So that by now each one of us is exposed to such an overdose of images each day of his life that it seems almost anachronistic to say as I just said: images have a potential for truth.[23]

The three primary reasons for the explosion in image production are the development of new and more efficient methods of reproducing images already mentioned; technical advances in the distribution of images; and the discovery of various ways in which images can be used to promote commercial interests. The most significant modern development that incorporates all three of these advancements is the invention of television and the technologies that subsequently stemmed from it, which Wenders sees as the main obstacle to establishing a culture of healthy visual perception.

Television and the commercialisation of images

The camera never lies: the photographic image is the provider of reliable, accurate and recognisable representations of reality which are widely trusted as authentic.

For the same reasons, photographic images can be a powerful tool of influence, in particular the cinema, which is available, and makes itself attractive, to the masses. The optical conditions that create an image on a negative film-strip inside a camera, the fact that light enters the camera through a lens and is projected, without further mediation, onto the negative, means that the camera really does never lie. (In the same vein, the temporal and spatial separation of an image on a photograph from the reality it depicts means that, in a sense, the camera always lies). The danger that this medium poses comes much more from the way the equipment is used, by whom and for what purpose, than from the photographic process itself. More than any other medium, film and photography are open to a kind of manipulation that is not the falsification of material reality itself, but the use of that reality for ulterior intentions. This circumstance threatens to pervert what Wenders considers cinema's duty: to give 'a true, valid and useful image of man in which he can not only recognise himself, but from which he can learn as well'.[24] Wenders' use of the term *Einstellung* in German, signifying both 'shot' and 'attitude', succinctly expresses this perceived connection between the mechanisms of cinematic production and the attitude a director has towards the physical reality that lies before the camera. This relationship determines – and can be evidenced in – how the given reality is transferred onto the screen, how it is presented to the spectator:

> Maybe not everyone will want to believe me; but I believe that each 'take' in a film also makes visible the 'take' on things of the man or woman who is responsible for it. Each 'take' shows you what's in front of the camera but also what's behind it. For me a camera is an instrument that works in two directions. It shows both object and subject. That's why in the end each 'take' shows the 'take' of the director.[25]

The director can choose, as Balázs describes, to show things 'as they are' (even though mediation through the film-maker is an inevitable and unavoidable factor), allowing the viewers to take part in the interpretation – or other receptional activity – of what they see. This idea rests on a perceived degree of respect towards what is in front of the camera and towards its accurate reproduction on the screen.[26] The intention to get as much reality onto the screen as possible means not just making images of a given reality, but also showing that reality in a way which allows its real nature to show through, which makes transparent the prevailing condition of the reality, showing things in a way that constructs a relation between the given reality and the life existing within it.

Or the director can choose to use images to try to force the spectatorship to some pre-calculated interpretation or conclusion based within the predefined limits of the film-maker's imagination. For Wenders, this is a question of how much freedom the film-maker allows the spectators to decide for themselves.

Amongst the most common subjects under discussion in Wenders' films are other media – music, the written word, but most particularly television. There is one visible in almost all of his films from *Same Player Shoots Again* to *The Million Dollar Hotel*. In many cases they are not working, their images are blank or else they have not even been unpacked, indicating that Wenders wants to use them thematically, but finds that what their screens show is not worth conveying to his own spectators. On the four occasions when we are allowed a clear picture of what is in the programme, they are other 'real' films – *Young Mr. Lincoln*, which is shown in one of Winter's motel rooms in *Alice in the Cities*, but it is constantly interrupted by advertising, and *The Chronicle of Anna Magdalena Bach* in the industrialist's villa in *Wrong Movement*. The first and fourth such occasions involve music, first in *Summer in the City*, then in *Until the End of the World*, where the rock group Talking Heads appear on the screen in an apparent reference to the classical Hollywood framing technique of the same name. With these four exceptions, the television image always seems to be blind and superficial, transporting nothing. Only in the two examples where images from another film are shown, or when a music-clip is shown, are the images clearly visible. Peter Buchka attributes Wenders' almost contemptuous treatment of television to its lack of

> utopian spirit, which is what constitutes the dignity of film. [Television] is not mocked because it's cinema's commercial enemy, but because it unconsciously multiplies cinema's false means. That makes video 'the cancer of images', as it is called in *Nicks Film: Lightning Over Water* ... Television and video may be growing phenomena, but their delusion of real life denies a mirror image of acute life.[27]

The commercialisation of images on one hand, and the inflation – or mass distribution – of commercial images through television on the other, results, if one accepts Jean Luc Godard's account of television's origins in Wenders' film *Chambre 666* (1982), from the fact that television 'was born at the very same time as the advertising that financed it. So it was the highly articulate advertising world that could say things in a single phrase or image, like Eisenstein, as good as Eisenstein, as good as Potemkin.'[28] The situation described by Godard has not changed significantly: in order to survive, private television stations are today compelled to compete for viewer attention

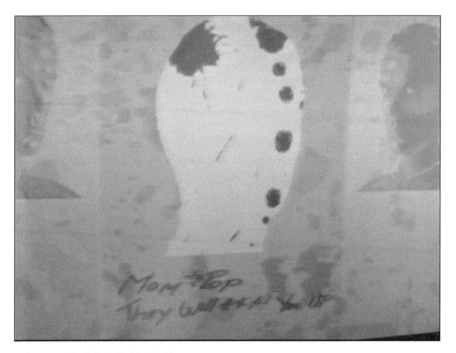

FIGURE 1   *Until the End of the World* (© 1991, Road Movies Filmproduktion GmbH)

through the programming they offer, and to maximise revenue from advertising in order to be able to provide the most appealing programmes. One outcome of this state of affairs in a competitive climate is an increase across the board in the amount of advertising distributed through television networks, whilst television has, at least until the development of the World Wide Web, provided the most effective advertising forum available to commercial bodies and institutions.

The commercial use of images in advertising and, more particularly, advertising in television gives Wenders, a director committed to promoting an open mode of perception sensitive to the underlying essence of physical existence, good cause for distress because television is such an efficient and effective distributor of images. He considers advertising a form of 'compulsion or violence', in that it always has the objective of promoting a specific idea, be it a product or a service. Advertising is incompatible with Wenders' concept of cinema, therefore, because his is a cinema based on minimising manipulation of the spectator to understand things in a certain way.[29]

[W]hen the film is ready, at the moment it's shown, compulsion exists inasmuch as there's a danger of it not allowing the audience the freedom to see something, but just telling them what they *have* to see. It's evident that that's a latent danger that films have. The extreme form of that is in commercials or propaganda films, where everything is done to ensure the viewer gets a certain message. That's extreme manipulation, and manipulation is violence or duress. Of course there are other films that show themselves to the viewer and leave him free to put the film together in his own way, and finally to determine which film he wants to see ... I try to get my films to be like that, so that they can exist in the imagination of each member of an audience, not forever pointing at something and saying; 'you're seeing this now, not something else!' 'That is the meaning of suchandsuch!' I try not to do so much finger-wagging and just leave the things there, so that you're free to see something or not, just as you are in life.[30]

Here, Wenders argues against the use of images for the transmission of information where the objective is to manipulate the spectator to understand the depicted reality in a certain way. The risk, he feels, is primarily that the image and the information transmitted through it might bear little or no natural relation to one another, causing a rift between signifier and signified.

The consequences Wenders draws from the phenomenon of image-based advertising, particularly in television, is that the mass distribution of such images may lead to a transformation of habitual visual perception, the fracturing of image and meaning, the dispersal of individuality, creativity, history, of the authentic which is dissolving in the pastiche of sounds and images generated by the modern communications media. Writing about his first visit to the US, Wenders describes how he feels images of all kinds characterise every aspect of life to the extent that even vision becomes eroded:

America, land of imagery. / Land made of images. / Land for images. / Even writing has become pictorial here.[31]
Why does this country need to advertise itself more than any other? [...] American television has only raised to a higher power this advertising campaign over the whole planet.[32]

In his film *Reverse Angle: NYC 1982*, he considers this practice to have led to a 'new age hostile to images (and an age of hostile images too)'.[33] Wenders feels that, far from providing images that might stem the rising tide of hostile images, new American films at the beginning of the 1980s also speak the language of television – of commerce – and are beginning to look like advertisements themselves:

There's no help from the cinema; on the contrary, new American films are looking more and more like trailers for themselves. So much in America tends to self-advertisement, and that leads to an invasion of and inflation of meaningless images. And television, as ever, at the forefront. Optical toxin.[34]

A novel by Emanuel Bove (*Mes Amis*) and a picture book of Edward Hopper's paintings remind him 'that the camera is capable of equally careful description, and that things can appear through it in a good light: the way they are'.[35]

Cinema films in television

Soon after the commercial introduction of television in the US in the 1950s, it found itself in competition with the cinema. In a bid to attract the American public out of the comfort of the living-room, the cinema attempted to develop ways of retaining interest in itself. It emphasised the 'physical superiority of its projected image in a series of technical "improvements" (Cinemascope, Widescreen, VistaVision, 3-D, etc.)',[36] and put its larger capital base to use in spectacular blockbuster productions.

However, Kracauer was already aware in 1960 that television was unlikely to kill off the cinema, and suggests three possible reasons for television's success, one of which is that television feeds on the products of the cinema, needing the survival of the cinema to ensure its own.[37] Television today looks to cinema for innovations and new ideas, as well as for entertainment material, making the cinema an 'area in which new styles of shooting and editing can be pioneered; and equally new forms of subject matter'.[38]

This act of scavenging, though, has since become sacrificed, in Wenders' opinion, for in order to reach the widest audiences and ensure financial success, cinema gave up its initial drive to compete with television and began instead to adapt to the formal conventions of the televisual image. This circumstance leads Wenders to complain that

cinema has always left more breathing space than television. In television these rules have tightened, just as the screen has shrunk. A clear example is when you watch films on TV. The spaces are no longer evident, say the wide shots in westerns. The rules have to be tighter because the viewer has to be tied to the thing more tightly. The cinema always kept this wonderful distance. But that's changing too now. New American films are just like television in the way they tie you to the screen. The loose bonds are getting tighter all the time.[39]

FIGURE 2   *Reverse Angle: NYC 1982* (© 1982, Road Movies Filmproduktion GmbH)

Television has had to find new ways of binding the viewer to the screen because its image is comparatively small. Typically, close-ups are much more frequent than in a cinema film in order for the details to be clearly visible on the small screen. Less attention is devoted to background detail for this reason. The visual impact of cinema films thus becomes compromised when they are shown on television.[40]

Television additionally appealed to its audience by matching cinema's offering of feature films and by sensationalising televisual events, keeping to a strict, reliable timetable that could encourage 'television appointments'. If these appointments were kept, then continued advertising revenue was guaranteed.

At the same time, Wenders claims, the public has accepted that, even in film, once an entirely separate medium from television, things must be in continuous movement. In interview with Leonetta Bentivoglio, he suggests that the rhythm of films today has changed since the introduction of television into daily life in the 1950s:

> I have the impression that ... when television was one thing and cinema another, and video didn't exist yet, one could watch a film much more attentively and patiently. Today, films have a completely different rhythm: they no longer dedicate much time to observing things, and neither does the public.[41]

This is an idea of television as a device that impedes freedom of vision because it focuses attention only on foreground details, and leaves little time for attentive observation of images because of the relatively fast cutting rhythms employed to offer constantly new and changing images, sensations and impressions to the viewers, lest they become wearied and switch to another channel. This is the same kind of manipulation of the audience that Wenders observes in advertising films. Films made for television must conform to these tighter rules because today's commercial cinema has a strong financial dependency on television:

> The financing of large-scale feature film production takes into account the eventual sale to TV ... The financing of radical, independent work also depends on TV financing ... Often, this dependence becomes excessive, as other possible sources of finance (state funding, private sources) tend to fade away, and the existence of a radical and independent sector becomes dependent on the internal decisions of a TV channel.[42]

This dependence, paradoxically, compromises cinema's ability to provide constant innovation, as Ellis describes, because television is required to be

> predictable and timetabled; it is required to avoid offence and difficulty ... The centrality of broadcast TV to everyday life combined with the resultant demands for timidity and predictability means that TV defines a kind of centre ground from which cinema, in a variety of ways, diverges. This centre ground is composed of TV's habitual attitudes and its habitual forms.[43]

With reference to Wenders' work and his position on the development of relations between modern cinema and television, the combination of, on the one hand, cinema's growing financial dependence on television with, on the other, television having adopted a centralist position, its dependence on advertising revenues and its worldwide dissemination of images has resulted in a dilution of the essence of individuality and identity of the objects depicted in its images: firstly because the mass reproduction of an individual object (or person) can compromise its uniqueness if it appears everywhere in images; secondly, because it can also appear outside its natural context; and thirdly, because any image, once produced and reproduced, can be used for the promotion of ideas, in advertising for example, to which the subject of the image has no natural connection. The attempts of film-makers to adapt to the viewing conditions television offers could lead, according to Wenders, to less challenging visual content in cinema films, thereby discouraging visual openness in perceptual habits generally:

> Nowadays it's mostly television that conserves images. But the inflation of electronic images offered us by television seems so unworthy of being recalled that you have to ask yourself whether it wouldn't be better to return to the old traditions of poets and painters. It's better to have a few images that are full of life than masses of meaningless ones. It's the vision that determines whether anything has been seen or not.[44]

In this chapter we have established that the photographic and filmic image is a commodity in great demand as an instrument of communication, the foremost reason for this being their ability to convince the viewer of the truth of the visual representation of the physical world contained within them. This latent truth potential, and the universal acceptability of filmic and photographic images makes them very powerful as mediators. But they are, for the same reasons, also very fragile and open to abuse. There are several ways in which the truth content they offer can, in a moral sense, easily be degraded or manipulated, foremost amongst these threats being story. This is the field of tension, openly thematised in Wenders' films and texts, in which the battle for dominance is fought.

The next chapter will explore the main reasons for Wenders' belief in this incompatibility of image and story in film by analysing how these two elements interact, and by investigating the various strategies Wenders employs to challenge or circumvent this conflict, and to emphasise the semantic force of the images in his films.

CHAPTER TWO

on the construction of narratives

Wenders discovered from the *Silver City* affair that it is difficult to speak of attaining a goal in film without also taking the question of narrative into consideration during planning and shooting. His proclaimed ideal of a cinema capable of re-establishing or preserving the integrity of the photographic image inevitably leads to certain questions: what role does the act – and the fact – of narration play in the selection of this goal; how do the laws and conventions of filmic narration influence the film-making process under these circumstances; how are they applied; and what, in Wenders' cinema, are the results?

Incompatibility of images and narrative

The opinion categorically expressed by Wenders that images and stories are mutually incompatible manifests itself in two different but interrelated ways in his films and in his utterances on the subject. His reaction to the inadvertent and unforeseen entrance of the man in *Silver City* focuses on the way a story can seem independently to assert its presence in a film against the will of the director. In this case, the suggestion of the existence of an unwanted story is a result of the temporal dimension inherent to the filmic medium, which allows the portrayal of action in film, and a result of the pre-conditioned nature of the average initiated film spectator who, familiar with conventional cinematic produce, is encouraged to expect some kind of causality from action in a film.

A second way in which Wenders expresses the incompatibility of images and stories in film is precisely the inverse of the situation in *Silver City*: that images must be manipulated if they are used to narrate a predefined story. This theory rests on Wenders' belief that the primary ability and role of images to show – due to their adherence to the appearance of physical reality – rather than tell – which involves the transmission of some kind of message – may be compromised if story is allowed to dominate in a film: '[Images] don't have it in them to be carthorses: carrying and transporting messages or significance or intention or a moral. But that's precisely what a story wants from them.'[1] If photographic images are forced into the frame of a predefined story, then the truth that is inherent to them by virtue of their 'photographic' nature risks being distorted. Such distortion of the empirical evidence that photographs provide therefore amounts to the negation of truth in a visual representation of reality.

Though this sounds like a bitter personal rejection of story in film, Wenders' sentiments are shared by other theoreticians such as Siegfried Kracauer. In his book, *Theory of Film*, Kracauer asserts that a film producer who deals with history or fantasy runs the risk of disavowing the basic character and nature of the medium. 'Roughly speaking, he seems no longer concerned with physical reality but bent on incorporating worlds which to all appearances lie outside the orbit of actuality.'[2] In Kracauer's formulation, one should understand fantasy as fiction of any kind, and under history, films of a dramatic nature rather than historical documentary.

To these, Wenders would add the current fashion in the US for re-makes of films as other types of filmic story that deny the documentary character of the photographic image, amounting to an abuse of images for the simple reason that they are appropriated to convey information with which their link is insubstantial. With a bold generalisation he directly criticises Americans for having a blind faith in their stories, to the extent that Hollywood continually recycles its stories.

> The American cinema today is feeding almost entirely off itself, dealing in experiences that only come out of other films. The connection between films and life, the notion that films deal with 'true-life experiences' is gone.[3]

Wenders refers to such films, specifically the most recent American films, as 'exercises in suppression' because they pervert the empirical evidence contained within the film images due to story being foregrounded,[4] claiming that this negates the real and original purpose of the cinema:

Of course, an entertainment film would like nothing better than to make you forget about the world. Entertainment means distraction from reality. But I think films were invented not to distract people from the world, but to point them back at it.[5]

Difficulties arise when the story of a film is more important than its images. Fiction (entertainment) films and historical dramas fall into this category by definition: fantasy and fiction are constructs of the imagination, while both fiction and historical drama films, even if they claim to be based on real or historical events, deny a vision of the contemporary material world. These genres may bear a relation to the contemporary world, but in view of Wenders' ideas of the cinema as an essentially image-based medium, this relation is oblique if the stories are so important that the images focus attention on the story, rather than on the content of the images. In this sense, the dominance of the narrative in a film – for what else is there to emphasise in fiction or drama – involves forcing the images into a frame that pre-exists the images:

> At the moment when a story no longer gives you direct access to things themselves, to the actual people, the city, the objects around, when everything has a function and a set role to play, and the story becomes the single overriding consideration, then I feel like I'm in a vacuum. ... But if the story is there first, and the story demands all my trust, then I'm unable to do anything with it. That's what happened to me in *The Scarlet Letter*, and the same thing happened in *Hammett* too.[6]

If direct access to things and persons is denied to the film-maker, if the underlying conditions of reality are mediated in film through the filter of a story, and if a film's narrative takes over the role from the image to act as the main information carrier as Wenders describes here, authority is detracted from the image. In Wenders' formulation of the priorities concerning cinematic expression, the relegation of the image to the role of supporting a less authoritative version of events – in fiction, this would be a version based in the fantasies of the imagination – risks perverting the value of the empirical evidence that a photograph offers. For Wenders, the function of the cinematic image as guarantor of an authentic visual representation of physical reality risks being compromised by the higher authority of the story, as might the motivation for making films at all. This is a notion that Wenders expresses in his film *Wrong Movement* through a speech made by the figure of Therese (Hanna Schygulla). As Therese, an actress, rehearses her lines for the next performance of a play, she stops to express regret that she must keep to her lines, ignoring the reality around her:

> I've just tried learning some lines of the play. Then I see this matchbox and wonder why it isn't in the play too. It's so artificial expressing oneself with other peoples' sentences.

Therese's speech succinctly expresses Wenders' attitude to reality in film: there is a risk that reality may be ignored because the film must follow a story, the all-important end of which insists that all irrelevancies are held at arm's length. They are part of a different reality from that of the film. Schygulla's words recall Wenders' comments after the making of *The Scarlet Letter*: 'I don't ever want to make another film in which a car or a petrol station or a television set or a phone booth aren't allowed to appear'.[7] This film was based on a novel by Nathaniel Hawthorn, and set in a seventeenth-century American village. Anything that was likely to seem out of tune with the ambience of a coastal village in seventeenth-century America had to be excluded from the artificial visual reality of the film. Yet Wenders still felt the urge to film a ship in the background, when their own ship was a cardboard cut-out hanging above the sea, or to film the actor Hans Christian Blech as he was filming the sea with an 8 mm camera during a break in the shooting.[8] The implication of Wenders' statement is that, in making a film based on a reality other than the reality of the film, the given reality is disregarded, and the most important function of film – to record visual phenomena accurately – may be jeopardised.

Just as with the image, then, Wenders insists that the story of a film is based on empirical evidence rather than on invented or imitated realities. This was what attracted him to Patricia Highsmith's novel *Ripley's Game* as a basis for his film *The American Friend*, as he states in his commentary to the film. Wenders admired the way Highsmith was able to draw a story out of the characters, rather than force a story on them, and that her stories, rather than being psychologising, are empirical – 'they never explain'.[9]

In each of the above cases, it is the lack of respect for the given reality that Wenders criticises, and in both cases he is talking about films that are based on other stories. The danger is that there is an increased risk of manipulation the further the image or story is distanced from a given reality, and in film, as it presents any given time as a present time, including historical films, the danger is considerable. In each case, too, the manipulation is for the purpose of dramatic effect or spectacle usually connected with dominant cinema. Or the other way around: the greater the degree of manipulation of the image to fit it into the frame of a predefined story, the less likely it is that the image or story will have a close relation to reality, and 'life', as Wenders expresses it, will ebb away from the images, or be sucked out of the images by the story as if by a 'vampire'.[10]

In this sense, it is interesting to compare reactions to the figures of the angels in *Far Away, So Close*. Despite them being fantasy figures, no critic has ever expressed incredulity at their characterisation, only at the background gangster story in the film. The angels are simply empirically present in the images, without needing to be justified. Critics and spectators alike are familiar with the concept of angels, and do not therefore need to question them as filmic figures, whereas the gangster story is a construct, a fiction considered weak by many critics because it does not conform exactly to the strict rules governing tension in the gangster/film noir genre, and because it feels like an artificially included episode in the film. With this in mind, the presence of Peter Falk may have been a gag: both in this film and in *Wings of Desire*, characters who meet Falk refer to him as 'Colombo', Falk's famous television detective personality, and express incredulity that it could really be him. They refuse to believe in Colombo's real existence, even though, or perhaps precisely because, they see him walking through the streets of Berlin. Colombo is too much a fiction to be real. Through this presentation of fiction in the frame of reality and of reality in the frame of fiction (the angels and Falk in both cases), Wenders is perhaps asking his spectators to reflect on which kind of story is the more probable: the existence of a real-life figure or the existence of a fantasy figure, to make the point that the expectations people have developed from fiction when it is presented as reality can lead to blindness when they are presented with a reality they connect primarily with a fiction.

Narrative as structure

> In films, the fiction, the story, is like the First Cause. Without it, sure, I could make documentaries, but I'm not really interested in that, I want to tell a story. The fiction gives me somewhere to be, it's what allows me to set up my camera at all.[11]

One of the paradoxes that characterises Wenders' work and theory is that the filmic story, which can suck the life from an image by suggesting connections where there are none, is what Wenders hopes will provide a coherent context for the presentation of his images: 'Right now too, without the brace of a story, images are starting to look interchangeable and purposeless to me',[12] he discloses in *Reverse Angle: NYC 1982*. This

FIGURE 3   *The State of Things* (© 1982, Road Movies Filmproduktion GmbH)

ambiguity has led the German publicist Norbert Grob to consider Wenders' attitude to narrative in film as 'Enthusiasm for stories, and mistrust of stories. In Wenders these are two sides of the same coin.'[13] The film-maker's position on story is initially mistrust because the images that are given the job of telling must be manipulated to fit the predefined route of the story. The images are thus called upon to convey meaning that is not inherent to them. By the time of *The State of Things*, however, he realises that some sort of story is necessary for the structure and existence of his films (rather than the assertion that 'enthusiasm', as Grob describes it, is a significant factor in Wenders' approach to story), and that they had always been present in his films as 'a hook for hanging pictures'.[14]

The State of Things represents Wenders' stand as a European director struggling to preserve the recognition of the artist in the face of dominant Hollywood-produced stories. In fact, it seems that Wenders is conscious from the beginning of the film that he has lost his battle against the giants of the American film industry, for it is in an interview covering this film that he admits to the potential advantages of having a story in his films, also in *The State of Things*, in order to hold the film together, to give the images and the story form and structure and to provide for some kind of narrative coherence. To the question, 'Is a story just the thread?' Wenders replies:

No, no, it's more than that. A story brings in structure. The story in *The State of Things* could have been left as a thread if Friedrich had just left his producer

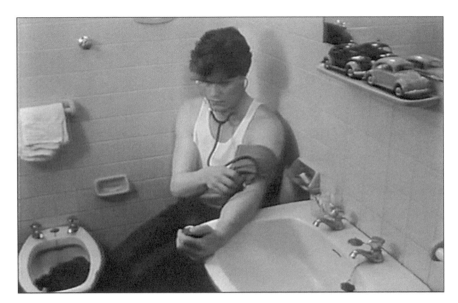

FIGURE 4   *The State of Things* (© 1991, Road Movies Filmproduktion GmbH)

riding around in his caravan: an open ending ... By making the story conclusive as opposed to inconclusive (by killing off the central figures), all the rest of it has also gained definition. So I've learned that I have to take on board story as structure, that I have to reacquire a dramaturgical language in order to be able to say everything else equally firmly.[15]

The necessity of a story in a film is alluded to in *The State of Things*: in an observing sequence, when the characters are filmed in the act of waiting for news from the financiers in the US, they are in a state of limbo, not able to produce anything of the planned film at all. In order to once again become active, they need to be given a story both by the director, Friedrich, and by their creator, Wenders. Without either of these they come to a complete standstill. Friedrich/Wenders does not want to admit a story into the space, but at the end of the film, Friedrich is killed by his creator because of the absence of a story in his film, 'The Survivors'. Wenders realises here that his film, *The State of Things*, was made possible only because it told an impossible rudimentary story:

> I came from images, I believed in a cinema of images. I thought a storytelling cinema was impossible. I only gradually began to realise that, in the end, my cinema of images could only exist because of the rudimentary stories they told.[16]

On the level of the required framework story in Wenders' films, the stories are usually based on one of two possible sources: real experiences of the director; or prescribed literary texts, usually novels. In both cases, the source allows for the creation of a fictional, sometimes pre-formulated story to act as a frame for the films that is also based in reality. The framework story in *Alice in the Cities*, for example, draws its shape from Wenders' first two visits to the US, first when he attended the American premiere of his film *The Goalkeeper's Fear of the Penalty Kick* and secondly when he made *Alice in the Cities*. He did not have a script to follow once he started shooting in Germany (the second half of the film) so the story developed out of movement. In *Kings of the Road*, Wenders used the discoveries he made during the filming of *Wrong Movement* and the journey made by the entire film crew along the East German/West German border. In *The State of Things* the story is based on Wenders' experiences during the production of *Hammett* in America, and the situation he found when he visited a director in Portugal to charitably deliver some black and white film stock to the stranded film-crew, whose finances were exhausted: their story became the background to the story for *The State of Things*, in which he films the crew – some of whom were borrowed from the real stranded crew – in the act of waiting. In *Nick's Film: Lightning Over Water*, Wenders and Ray had intended to begin where *The American Friend* had left off, to which the establishing sequence as Wenders gets out of a taxi and goes up the stairs to Ray's apartment, and Ray's commentary, testify. Instead, they used the reality of Ray's illness and Wenders' desire to hold up the disappearance forever of one of the film-makers who had most influenced his own film-making as the given reality, from which they then prepared a story – the story of this reality. 'Everything that happens, says Wenders, had been set out and written down beforehand by him and Ray. They never had a story, so their reality became their story.'[17]

By the time of *Wings of Desire*, the situation becomes more complex, but even here, the narrative is structured from the vision and hearing of the angels, whose perceptive capabilities mirror those of the film camera and the microphone. *Arisha, the Bear, and the Stone Ring* (1992) documents a journey from Berlin to the north-east German island of Rügen, a journey on which characters that make up the fabric of German society are encountered by the bear (Rüdiger Vogler) and Santa Claus (Wim Wenders), encounters that are filmed on video by Wenders himself. Finally, *Lisbon Story* tells the story of a film-sound technician, Philip Winter (Rüdiger Vogler again) discovering the Portuguese capital through his work – a parallel to Wenders' original intention to make a documentary film on the city.

These stories (although all are, strictly speaking, fictional) are based on real experiences, and are usually the product of movement or of involvement in events.

They therefore resemble those types of story that Kracauer defines as 'found' in the following terms:

> all stories found in the material of actual physical reality. When you have watched for long enough the surface of a river or a lake you will detect certain patterns in the water which may have been produced by a breeze or some eddy. Found stories are in the nature of such patterns. Being discovered rather than contrived, they are inseparable from films animated by documentary intentions.[18]

Their link – through their basis in physical reality and Wenders' experience of it – with the documentary tradition means that found stories mirror events and things taken from a real given environment. In film, this depends on their link with the photographic images that Wenders so faithfully trusts to authentically reproduce visual reality. For in film, the images are first and foremost instruments that mediate between physical reality itself, and the story that those images tell. For Wenders, the found story is thus the ideal narrative form because the given environment is respected. His favoured filming method has, time and again, been to search out locations that raise images in his mind.

In the cases when literary texts function as outlines for the films (*The Goalkeeper's Fear of the Penalty Kick, Wrong Movement, The American Friend,* and *Wings of Desire*) the situation is similar: in the first, Wenders claims to have been primarily interested in how one thing followed into another, sentence to sentence, rather than in the development and progress of the story, meaning that he was most interested in the structure of the novel which, he says, reads like a film script.[19] In *Wrong Movement,* Wenders changed Handke's script somewhat, except for the dialogues, and attempted to imitate the novel 'in its "naturalistic" descriptive tendencies, its observation of minute details'.[20] In both *Paris, Texas* and *Wings of Desire,* the scripts were only there to provide the dialogues, and so the stories were invented or found. In the former, Harry Dean Stanton allowed his real biography to be used for the character of Travis in the film,[21] which Wenders describes as 'an almost empty narrative structure ... filled in by the actors and by pooling all our experience. Discover the story, in other words. It's the only way I can do it now. And there's no better way of making an adventure film.'[22] All of these examples suggest that Wenders was primarily interested in the texts for the structure they provided, or because they were based on real experiences, with the possible exception of Highsmith's *Ripley's Game,* and the story of Travis in *Paris, Texas,* which he chose because he felt that the story was extracted from the characters, rather than imposing itself on them.

Story as 'vampire'

Time and again, Wenders alludes to the concept of story as 'vampire' by imposing stories on his characters that they do not necessarily want to be involved in. The most prominent example is *The State of Things*, in which Friedrich, a film director (Patrick Bachau), struggles to complete his film because the funds are not forthcoming from his shady financiers across the Atlantic in Los Angeles. In the end, he tries to find Gordon, his producer (Allen Goorwitz), but discovers that the financiers are already on Gordon's tail, and he is hiding out in a mobile home. Against Hollywood conventions, Friedrich had decided to make his film in black and white because 'life is in colour, but black and white is more realistic', as his colleague Joe (Sam Fuller) explains in Portugal. But Friedrich and Gordon's discussion takes on the theme of narrative in a more philosophical fashion. Friedrich/Wenders admits to the belief that 'stories only exist in stories'. Gordon, however, asserts that 'a film without a story is like a house without walls'.

This attitude, which reflects the narrative tendencies of dominant, mainly American, cinema, contrasted with Friedrich's reply that 'the [visual] space between the characters is enough to carry the film', does, as Wenders himself confesses, represent his dilemma concerning story in film. But it also refers more specifically to his experience in Los Angeles while making *Hammett*, produced by Francis Ford Copolla. On Copolla's insistence, the film had to be re-scripted three times, re-edited and re-filmed several times and presented before a sample audience to judge their views before it was considered fit for the market, and for the Orion Pictures studios, who were expecting more of an action film than one centred on the figure of the writer.[23] Friedrich and Gordon in *The State of Things* are eventually caught up and murdered by the financiers and, paradoxically, Friedrich is killed at the end of a story whose allusion to film noir is all too obvious, and that he had been trying to avoid telling in Portugal. The story in this film becomes a thriller which bleeds the life out of its protagonists. What is left at the end of the story are the images which, like photographic images, are concrete enough to carry the real story in the film about two different and seemingly mutually excluding ideas of cinema: cinema as art, and cinema as commerce.

Wenders again alludes to the seductive powers of the Hollywood story in *The American Friend*. Jonathan Zimmermann (Bruno Ganz) is a picture framer in Hamburg who learns that he has a fatal illness. Ripley (Dennis Hopper) is a shady American art dealer who travels back and forth between the US and Germany, and who has connections with an organised crime ring. Knowing of Jonathan's illness, a ringleader offers him a sum of money if he will assassinate an enemy in Paris. Jonathan is a family man and the least likely person one would expect to involve himself in a murder, but after initial doubts he accepts the offer, justifying his decision with the promise of leaving his family some money when he dies. While it is not the case, as Kolker and Beicken suggest, that Ripley actively offers Jonathan a 'movie-like life of intrigue, assassination and gangster martyrdom',[24] there is no doubt that the middle-class, bourgeois Jonathan is attracted by Ripley's apparent rootlessness and suspicious dealings, of which he is well aware from the beginning of the film. The character of Ripley is based on dominant cinematic codes 'that have colonised our subconscious', claims Filippo D'Angelo,[25] recalling Bruno Winter's famous phrase from *Kings of the Road*. Reinhold Rauh's opinion of this phrase as a possible cryptic interpretation of *The American Friend* seems justified because, from this point of view, Jonathan's consciousness seems so colonised by the myth of the glamorous Hollywood story that he is seduced, against his instinct, but in accordance with his will – his dreams, perhaps – to enter such a story with himself in the lead role.[26] He looks lost and out of place in the glossy, futuristic ambience of the Paris Metro. In terms of Wenders' description of the filmic story as vampire, D'Angelo makes perhaps the most astute point that would seem to confirm the notion of seduction:

> European cultural dependence on American cinema is a link that becomes a metaphor for the wider relationship between spectator and film. If Tom [Ripley] is the Cinema, full of fascination and power, then Jonathan is his Spectator, the individual seduced by the magic of the medium, transported into a fantastic dimension far removed from reality.[27]

Like a vampire, the story that entwines Jonathan slowly sucks the life remaining in him out of his body, and at the end of the film, he dies. His adventure provided only the temporary realisation of a dream long cultivated through the dominance of Hollywood's stories and images.

A third significant allusion to the concept of story in film as vampire is Wenders' fictional role as the film director in *Nick's Film: Lightning Over Water*. Wenders/the director uses (up) the life of the Ray/the character to realise his own film. In the course of time, Ray's life ebbs away in order that work on the film can continue. This allusion suggests that, in creating fiction out of reality, the cinema destroys the objects it uses, thereby exhausting its material. Ray dies in front of the camera because he knows that the film will transfer his vitality, his gestures, from reality onto celluloid, to perpetuate them in time. On the other hand, the film shows Wenders to be like Ripley in *The American Friend*, who uses the life of a friend egotistically while, in a way, prolonging his life.

Road movies and episodic narrative structure

As opposed to mainstream cinema, Wenders (like some of his colleagues of the New German Cinema, for example Jean-Marie Straub, Werner Nekes, and Werner Herzog) moves away from conventional patterns of plot construction in his films and towards an episodic narrative structure in order to grant his films a degree of coherence that a story can offer, while at the same time respecting the role and integrity of the image as the chief carrier of information. Just as Philip Winter's story in *Alice in the Cities*, which he tells Alice in the Wuppertal hotel to help her sleep, is a series of episodes related in an 'and then ... and then...' fashion, so too are Wenders' films constructed as chains of relatively autonomous events: autonomous in that individual episodes usually only lead from one to the next because they are placed there during editing, rather than for reasons of cause and effect or for psychological motives. Kracauer observes the same tendency in the silent comedies of early cinema in which the stories often served as a frame for slapstick pranks:

> What matters is that the units follow each other uninterruptedly, not that their succession implements a plot. To be sure, they frequently happen to develop into a halfway plausible intrigue, yet the intrigue is never of so exacting a nature that its significance would encroach on that of the pieces composing it.[28]

Rather than serving exclusively to further the progress of a story, the scenes, sequences, or shots can serve to build an episodic narrative structure when they follow one another as a sequence of events. Although such an individual sequence can bear a relation to other sequences in a film, the importance of each sequence in itself as an autonomous unit is preserved, as Kracauer emphasises. Only if this characteristic is fulfilled can such a unit be defined as episodic. The result for Wenders' cinema is that he takes care to remain, as much as possible, faithful to the temporal and spatial dimensions of such unitary scenes, most particularly in the early years. This involves avoiding the temptation to use editing for expressive or dramatic effect. Already in his first 16mm film, *Schauplätze*, Wenders filmed a road junction without moving the camera or switching it off until the reel was empty. 'With hindsight, I suppose it would have seemed like sacrilege to me.'[29] Similarly, in the extremely contemplative *Silver City*, each of the film's sequences is uncut, and lasts as long as a full reel of film. In this way, single events tend to keep their individual character because, rather than contributing directly to the progress of a story, they are strung together like beads on a necklace: each episode retains its uniqueness. This gives the early films a very fragmented atmosphere, in which events are not composed with the specific intent of nearing the end of a prescribed route. The telling of a story is thus not the immediate objective of the films; rather, the story is an integral part of the act of filming, one that does not necessarily serve any specific goal. Referring to his school film *Same Player Shoots Again*, Wenders discusses the sequence with the man limping across the screen: 'You see only the man's legs and you know that he's been wounded because he loses some blood. But you don't know what's before and after.'[30] This film begins by suggesting a standard narrative, but this is soon abandoned first when the music soundtrack suddenly stops, then through the six-fold repetition of the sequence. Again, one sequence in *Summer in the City* is eight minutes long, 'as long as it took to drive the whole of the Kurfürstendamm in Berlin.'[31] As radical as these long shots were, their main effect in relation to time is not only to stress film's ability to capture events unfolding in their real time, but also to stress that this is just a snippet of a larger whole that had an existence before the beginning of filming, and continues after it. Film's own technical limitations therefore stress the act of filming as an act of documenting the fleeting nature of the passage of time in these examples: an episode is, by definition, only a selected part of a greater, ongoing process or sequence of events that can nevertheless be considered to be an independent unit.[32]

In Wenders' films, the open form functions as a component part of the episodic narration. Just as Alice falls asleep before Winter finishes his tale in *Alice in the Cities*, which has no recognisable ending, so Wenders' films often do not seem to come to, or even to seek, a conclusive state of affairs. The absence in Wenders' films of specific points at which one can say that the stories begin and end frequently gives rise to the impression that the cameras or characters simply arrive and leave during the progress of a narrative that originates beyond the temporal and physical boundaries of the filmic narrative, potentially having been involved in a story elsewhere, or already seeking a next story. Philip Winter in *Alice in the Cities* simply sits on a beach at the end of the story of his journey across the USA. Robert in *Kings of the Road* charges his car into the river Elbe at the end of his story with his family in Genoa. Travis in *Paris, Texas* is introduced as someone who has committed acts of violence in the recent past. None of these stories are shown, but they instead give the story we see an angle. As a document of the passing of time, Wenders' cinema only captures tiny fragments of life and existence. Such stories have a close relation with physical existence because, due to their open ends and open beginnings, they acknowledge the temporal and physical limitations of the medium, stressing that the films do not pretend to catch more than just an extract of the larger, ongoing story or event. Perhaps a parallel can be made with Pasolini's concept of '*kino in natura*' which characterises cinema as an endless and continuous sequence of shots recorded by an invisible and virtual camera, the 'written language of reality' of which films are a component part:

> The difference between cinema and film, all films, is that cinema possesses the *analytical* linearity of an endless and continuous sequence of shots, while films possess a potentially endless and continuous, but *synthetic* linearity.[33]

This tendency in Wenders' cinema to apply the open form is undoubtedly related to Wenders' early reluctance to use the cut – his preference for allowing things to continue until the film reel runs out, which avoids the necessity of imposing a too-obviously constructed narrative structure on his films. In seven of his seventeen full-length feature films the camera flies into the beginning of the narrative with the aid of a helicopter or a jet-aircraft, though this is sometimes preceded by a short prologue (as in *Wings of Desire*, which begins with images of a hand writing a poem, in *The End of Violence*, which features as its first images a film-set in Los Angeles, and in *The Million Dollar Hotel*, which begins with an introduction narrated by the main protagonist, Tom Tom). Those films are *Wrong Movement, Paris, Texas, Wings of Desire, Far Away, So Close, Beyond the Clouds* (Wenders was responsible for prologue and epilogue),[34] *The End of Violence* and *The Million Dollar Hotel*. Additionally, the first shot of *Alice in the Cities* features an aircraft in flight, and *Until the End of the World* begins with a view from outerspace of the sun rising on the earth, immediately followed by aerial landscape sequences. *Summer in the City, Kings of the Road, Nick's Film: Lightning Over Water, The American Friend,* and *Lisbon Story* all begin with a character's arrival on the scene by car, or with a car journey, and *The Scarlet Letter* begins with the arrival of Chillingworth (Hans Christian Blech) on the New England coast by sea. Both this film and *Far Away, So Close* end with boat journeys out of the area of the diegesis, *Nick's Film: Lightning Over Water, Alice in the Cities, Summer in the City, The End of Violence,* and *The Million Dollar Hotel* end with air journeys out of the diegetical space, in *Kings of the Road* and *Paris, Texas* the characters drive away and *Until the End of the World* ends as it started, with Claire looking down at the Earth from space.

In all the above cases, the films begin and end with the arrival or departure of either the characters or the camera in the diegetical space, giving the spectator the impression of dropping in on a story already in progress, rather than there being any question of how or when these stories began – a tactic to weaken the authority of story in Wenders' films. Of the eighteen features, only *The State of Things* can be said to have an identifiable beginning and ending – precisely the very film in which Wenders' crisis over the role of story in film reaches its peak. *The Goalkeeper's Fear of the Penalty Kick* is the only other exception to the tendency for the films to begin in flight, yet even here, there is no sense of a conventional story having begun: the football-match sequences with which the film both begins and ends are, again, little more than prologue and epilogue to the protagonist's journey.

Seen as a series of episodes without end, due to the inter-linkage of one film with the next, it becomes, in Norbert Grob's opinion, questionable whether a story is told at all:

> In real life, stories happen, just like that. Only those who experience it also know about it. But it only becomes graspable when it has reached its end. Only then can it be told as a story. The ending defines the intimate binding of the events. Because only the death of the story gives each individual event the meaning that it adopts for the purpose of the story.[35]

An episodic narrative structure, where the episodes follow one another, finds its natural ally in the road movie genre, with its emphasis on constant movement along a narrative trajectory. Conversely, films can be episodically structured without necessarily being road movies, such as *Wings of Desire* – an experiment in episodic narrative structure.

One of the features of Wenders' films is the open, episodic narrative form: a strategy to minimise the dominance of story in a film as well as the similarity of their narratives to conventional filmic narration. Establishing shots, conventionally used in dominant cinema to introduce the space in which the story of the film will unfold, including films with an episodic structure, is one of the foundations of conventional filmic narration. Often there are several establishing shots in films, which punctuate the progress of the story to link action, dialogue, or emotions with certain locations, or to furnish the spectator with exegetic information pertaining to a sequence before it begins. Regarding the open form of Wenders' films, in particular the road movies, the fact that the story unfolds, by definition, on the road renders such establishing shots less effective as a way of beginning a story since there are likely to be several stations along the road equal in importance to the first. The probable consequence is that each station, unless it is entered during travel, would require an establishing shot of its own. This is rarely the case in Wenders' road movies because it is more usual for his characters to enter a location during their travels, accompanied by the camera, thus reducing the need for conventional establishing shots. Those feature films that cannot be classified as road movies, however (*The American Friend*, *The State of Things*, *Paris,*

Texas, Wings of Desire, Far Away, So Close, Lisbon Story, The End of Violence, The Million Dollar Hotel), are strongly associated with the locations in which they are set and, correspondingly, have establishing shots that emphasise location (New York, Sintra, Berlin, Lisbon and Los Angeles). The minimisation of narrative dominance achieved by the episodic structure is augmented by the combination with the road movie genre, in that the traditional introduction to a narrative space that establishing shots provide – including those in Wenders' non-road movies, whether they conform to an episodic structure or not – is transformed into a sequence or shot that holds little more weight than any other sequence or shot in the films. This effect is similar to the way that the episodic structure, consisting of a string of consecutive occurrences, diminishes the narrative peaks of an individual event.

A road movie, a story that unfolds on the road, firstly has a greatly expanded diegetical space and, secondly, this space includes – which is not always the case in episodic narrative films – the space covered during travel. Sometimes in Wenders' films, the movement itself between two locations is not documented. In a film such as *Until the End of the World*, this very fact becomes a narrative element in that it is a projection of travel as it may seem at a future time, namely, that it will be so effortless and so fast that great distances can be covered in little time, and the fact of travel itself no longer gives rise to impressions as it did, for example, in *Kings of the Road*. Conversely, when all transport modes are knocked out by a nuclear accident at the beginning of the second half of *Until the End of the World*, and when the characters travel through lesser-developed countries in the film such as Russia and China, travel becomes painfully slow once more, and the characters again experience space as time and encounter stories, characters and events, just as Robert and Bruno had in *Kings of the Road*.

In all of Wenders' road movies, however, the fact of constant motion means that the diegetical space is always changing. Especially when the characters feel at home on the road, they are at the same time distanced from the environment they pass through because they rarely become involved in any precise geographical location to the extent that a rapport develops with it, or that the time they spend there can metamorphose from being just an episode to forming a recognisable story. Instead, the characters pass through a landscape which they observe from within a vehicle – whether it is above the clouds in an aircraft or across an ocean – and which we, the spectators, observe together with them. The landscapes have the function, usually, of characterising the figures' inner states by association. The fact that they merely pass through these environments is often of significance for character identification: motion means, for Winter, Robert and Wilhelm Meister in the trilogy *Alice in the Cities, Wrong Movement* and *Kings of the Road*, avoiding any kind of intimacy and integration with a town, a rural population or any particular environment apart from the constantly changing road and the inside of the vehicle. In none of the road movies do the characters ever return to the same location twice. In a traditional narrative film, however, there is usually a place or centre that is decisive for the protagonists or for the story, be it a ranch in the wild west, a space-station, a detective bureau, or a family home. Wenders' road movies progress along a narrative trajectory that, even when it does not necessarily follow a straight line, never doubles back on itself. Instead, figures are never at home, break away from home onto the open road, live in a mobile home on the road, use someone else's home as a transit point, or live in hotels. Although many of these characters do, in fact, depart from or visit a location that might be considered a family base, their time there has no significance other than, usually, as a catalyst to move away.

The situation is quite different if one examines those films of Wenders that one cannot classify as road movies. Although Jonathan Zimmermann travels to Paris and Munich on contract for a criminal organisation, the story centres around his home town of Hamburg, his family apartment, his workshop, and Ripley's home. The angels in *Wings of Desire* and *Far Away, So Close* move around Berlin, but always between the same few familiar locations of the public library, the Siegessäule column, and a film-set in the former and, additionally in the latter, Damiel's '*Pizzeria Del Angelo*'.

The road movie genre, then, contributes in Wenders' films to the weakening of narrative dominance already achieved through the episodic construction of the narrative, in that the potential for familiarity with any of the locations in which the episodes are set to develop is, both for the character and for the spectator, diminished due to their status as transitory stations along an unrelenting narrative trajectory. This is particularly true when, as in Wenders' earlier films, many of the episodes cover the act of travelling itself. The traditional narrative film depends on points of reference, often determined in establishing shots such as the examples already mentioned, to establish a sense of the spatial factors at play in the filmic story, or perhaps to disclose some relevant details about a place or character, if these are of narrative importance. But the fact that Wenders' road movies are, by definition, set on the road, means that they lack geographic points of reference that have relevance for narrative closure. Every physical or geographical point of reference has narrative relevance only in that they are passed through like dots on a road map – which, according to Wenders, often plays the greatest role in determining the scripts of his films – or in that they have something to do with the development of the central figures. But almost never do these locations contribute to the progression of the narrative to a conclusive ending. They are, and remain, little more than points on a map preserved in the films' images, rather than in their narratives, which almost forces an episodic structure on the films.

Understatement of dramatic highlights

Wenders hopes the story that inevitably develops from the act of showing images consecutively will not become more important than the images themselves. But he also actively tries to avoid the 'vampire narrative' that uses up the images through maintaining a tight control over the development of dramatic tensions and influences. In *The Logic of Images*, Wenders asserts his belief that images are able to stand on their own without necessarily leading to something else.[36] This shows just how much Wenders is influenced by the specific aesthetics of photography rather than of the film-image. Indeed, in his early years as a film student, the observing tendency his films exhibited and promoted – from *Schauplätze* to *Summer in the City* – often seemed to exclude the possibility of interference by a story, and the images (and, equally, the sound) were charged with carrying both the meaning of the films and, in the few cases that had one, with developing their narratives. *Same Player Shoots Again*, for instance, is peculiarly void of action of any kind, yet the allusion to the gangster genre through the soundtrack, the card-game, the great-coat and the machine-gun raise in the spectator the expectations of action and narrative. In fact, a story is only suggested through the observation of 'after action', *temps morts*, that only hint that some event may have taken place just before the arrival of the observing photographer. The greater part of the film is made up of a single sequence that is repeated. Initially, one assumes from the *mise-en-scène* that a gangster has been injured in a gun battle because he limps across the picture from right to left, carrying a weapon, but after the fifth repetition of the sequence one doubts whether the suggestion of a story initially perceived has anything at all to do with the purpose of the film. The multiple repetition of this scene – which, in each repetition, differs only in the colouring of the celluloid – would suggest instead that the aim was simply to contemplate the images, or perhaps look for a difference between each repetition. But at no time is there a suggestion that the director is interested in influencing one's interpretation: rather, he suggests the existence of a story but in the same breath asserts that he will not be the one to tell it. That is left very much for the spectator to arrive at. Just like with a photograph, the director's objective is simply to observe and compose a scene for the sake of the images that the scene suggests – images that the viewers would have been familiar with from their assumed experience and knowledge of the gangster genre – and to offer this view to the spectators, transferring to them the option to see a story – or not.

Concordant with this is the tendency to understate dramatic highlights in order to diffuse the development of a strong narrative and to maintain a focus on ordinary events. This was already a feature of Wenders' school films, for example *Alabama: 2000 Light Years From Home*, which has a perceivable beginning, middle and end, but actual events that conform ordinarily to the crime genre are not shown, just suggested. The gangster who has to kill another gangster is merely given a gun and told, 'You know what to do.' The spectator is then witness only to his drive to the destination where he must carry out his duty, and his drive again from it, during which he seems to black out at the wheel and, apparently, dies as a result of a gun-shot wound at the end of the film. This enables the telling of a story without adhering to the conventions of the genre, that is, without resorting to making things plain. In this way, observation and suggestion, relying on spectator familiarity with the rules and customs of the gangster genre, allow the suggestion of the existence of a story without actually telling a story. Wenders himself described *Alabama: 2000 Light Years From Home* in interview as 'a story, and not a story'.[37]

The Italian film critic Filippo D'Angelo refers to *The Goalkeeper's Fear of the Penalty Kick* to show how, through understating the protagonist's murder of the cinema's cashier girl, the absence of dramatic tension usually connected with – and imposed by – the standards is made plain:

> Bloch puts the belt of a dressing gown around the girl's neck: this is just an insignificant act – like a game – just one of the character's actions. An uncontrollable impulse then makes him complete the action and he strangles her. It is such an unexpected and casual act ... that makes the absence of dramatic tension, demanded by the constitutive standards of the [suspense] genre, clearer.[38]

The camera remains fixed in a wide-angle view, refusing to isolate any other detail from the overall scene. The murder is normalised as a part of the continuum of the diegesis, having no privileged position in the dramatic development of the film.

Again bending the rules of the genre, but in the opposite direction, Wenders uses music to build up tension in *Lisbon Story* when there is no real reason for it. Philip Winter is on the search for his friend Friedrich Monroe in Lisbon, but the music soundtrack suggests that something sinister has become of him. From the point of view of the plot, this serves to, somewhat ironically, overstate the dramatic tension.

When the friend is found, his reaction – to greet Winter heartily, and continue talking about his film project – diffuses all dramatic tension that had built up, also in Winter, without reason. In this case, the highlight is Winter's search for Friedrich – which complements the film's purpose to document the city of Lisbon – rather than the finding of the friend.

Wenders considers films that only tell the affirmative type of story, the highlights, as 'a kind of lying stunt. Reduced to that, storytelling is just froth'.[39] In order not to detract importance from the other scenes in a film, or from the primary objective of observing physical reality, Wenders de-emphasises dramatic high-points and, occasionally, emphasises points empty of real drama, or points that are meant for pure observation through long sequences in which the narrative development is forgotten for a moment. For Wenders, the telling of a story should not just focus on the highlights, but should, if a story must be told at all, include everything there is to tell or to see, as Hanns, his character in *Summer in the City*, suggests: 'One year in jail, one year to tell it.'

By making the image the basis of his cinema, and giving every sequence, not just the dramatic highlights, equal status, Wenders constructs a narrative system that denies narrative development to the point of it becoming dominant. Individual sequences are thus encouraged to stand alone, having a value in themselves. The same can often be said about single shots. In many cases, action is suggested but not shown, making his aesthetic one of observation of 'no action' events as well. This mode of film-making enables Wenders, whose interest is to make films about the time in which he lives, to extend the physical space of the story from the predefined limits of a prepared script or a novel which, if the telling of those stories are the focus of the film, may tend to diminish the freedom to overstep the boundaries of the prescribed work.

Temporal dilation in the filmic story

The above analysis does not mean to say that Wenders' films are completely void of action and drama. On several occasions Wenders has subjected his characters to dramatic situations, as if to test the strength of his argument against driving a story to its end, a story that moves from one highlight to the next; for example in *The American Friend*, *The State of Things* and *Far Away, So Close*. Each time, the character becomes involved in some sort of story, is allowed to experience life as a series of highlights and falls victim to the 'vampire narrative'. In each case, these stories stand out as individual episodes in the films in which they occur, but differ from the bulk of the films' episodes in that there are points at which they clearly begin and end; they are closed episodes that cover a specific and pre-determined period of time. Wenders' main achievement in these experiments with story is to illustrate the effect of temporal manipulation on how time is experienced when the story follows a prescribed narrative route to its inevitable end, in comparison with the open form to which the rest of the respective films and their episodes adhere, when one episode is usually no more a highlight than the next.

Jonathan Zimmermann in *The American Friend* was the first of Wenders' characters, apart from some protagonists of the school films, to be seduced by the vampire narrative. Before Ripley appears, Jonathan's is a quiet, domestic family life without obvious drama or excitement. The fantasy role of under-cover assassin offered by his 'American friend' is a briefly attractive proposition for Zimmermann. He succumbs to the temptation to enter the world of film noir as a gangster but, once he takes his decision, the story he becomes involved in must also find its end. Time runs out for Zimmermann, and his story inevitably dies with him after three dramatic murders and a dramatic escape from other gangsters.

In *The State of Things* the situation is somewhat different: here, Friedrich and his film-crew are stranded on the Portuguese coast, lacking the money and the material to continue the shoot. They are lost in a temporal standstill. There is neither a story to be filmed, nor a story in the film. The 'American friend' in this case is the financier of Friedrich's film who insists on the film having a strong story. From the moment Friedrich lands in America, time begins to run faster in the film and another gangster drama begins. The detective movie elements – the search for Gordon, the car-chase sequences and the shooting – push the film on to the end, and to its death. This story, once it moves to America, also becomes a series of highlights. Wenders expresses his motive for having Friedrich shot at the end of the film in the following terms:

> This film, that proposed the theory that 'storytelling is impossible in cinema', only exists because it tells a little story. In the end, this miserable little story disproved this theory. That's why I had the director shot at the end. And then I thought, if this miserable mini-story, this little shred of a story can hold the film together, then why not try it the other way around, then we'll see whether or not you can rely on a story.[40]

Most particularly, Cassiel's story in *Far Away, So Close* makes a strong link between the death of the character, the story, and the forward motion of time in a filmic story. Just as in *Wings of Desire*, the angel Cassiel and his colleagues occupy a timeless zone in which no action is possible. Cassiel's passage from angelic to human existence involves a shift in temporal conditions and allows action to take place which, in both Damiel's and Cassiel's cases, results in the birth of a story. Once Cassiel becomes a human, which is induced by accident, temporal flow begins to take effect as his story develops, again, into a gangster drama. Cassiel enters into a close relation with a new 'American friend' in this story (time is personified in the film in the character of Emit Flesti (Willem Dafoe), whose name is 'Time Itself' spelt backwards). When Flesti is around, the ticking of a clock is constantly audible in the background. He repeatedly looks at his pocket watch, but it has no face: he seems fascinated by the movement of the clockwork mechanism inside. He introduces himself to Cassiel in the following fashion:

> In the beginning there was no time. After a moment, time began with a splat … There's a word on your forehead Cassiel, written with tears. It's a word for loss, describing someone who wanted to see paradise from the outside and never found his way back, a word waiting to appear, one day, just for the tiniest moment.

Later in the film we discover that this word is 'so long'.

From the moment he becomes human, Cassiel is pressed on by Flesti. Cassiel's guardian angel Raphaela (Nastassja Kinski) herself reiterates in her monologue that 'To everything there is a season' yet when time threatens the newly-born Cassiel, who complains that 'everything goes by so fast', she begs Flesti in vain not to intervene in Cassiel's progress through time. 'Old hunters never die', she says to Flesti, who retorts, 'They just fade away. But not me. Never.' It is Flesti who encourages Cassiel to gamble in the underground station, for which he lands in jail. He introduces him to schnapps, and Cassiel becomes a drunkard. Finally, Flesti leads Cassiel to the place where he is to die, but in the moment of Cassiel's death, Flesti appears to show compassion in that he symbolically stops time – in fact, he stops the motion of a giant pulley-wheel in the mechanism of the barge lift that is raising the canal-boat holding the hostages taken captive by Russian arms dealers – to enable the young girl, Raissa, to escape from their clutches and the circus troupe to overpower the criminals. With Cassiel's death, action stops and for him, time, the necessary condition for action (and stories) to occur, is frozen. But this is also a necessary condition to enable Cassiel to return from the restrictive human time dimension into the dilated time of the angels. Time stops with the death of Cassiel – his short human existence, his story, comes to an end.

Yet for Cassiel, who constantly worries 'Why can't I be good?', the only thing that mattered was this story, in which he twice saved the life of a young girl. That was the highlight of his life, the only thing that, in the end, makes it worth living for Cassiel.

But perhaps the most crucial sequence in all of Wenders' work that confronts the vampire narrative, which sucks the life out of characters in the relentless drive towards the end of the story, with Wenders' tactic to weaken narrative dominance through de-emphasis of dramatic highlights in an episodic narrative structure, is represented by the scene when Cassiel meets Winter. In this elaborate scene, Wenders alludes to his film *Kings of the Road* through Winter's dying words. It is reasonable to assume that this is the same Winter as Bruno Winter in the former film, because of the evident inter-linkage between Wenders' films: in this case, the name and character of Winter. In *Kings of the Road*, with its open-ended, episodic narrative structure, Winter expresses his satisfaction at having, for the first time, the feeling that he has a story: 'I suddenly see myself as someone who has lived through a time, and that time is my history. It's a comforting thought.' It is in *Far Away, So Close*, though, where Winter's travels seem to come to an end when he is shot through the heart by Flesti. His last words are a direct reference to his speech as Bruno Winter, and reflect his twenty-year career as Wenders' favourite character and alter-ego:

I'm searching, as usual. I found nothing, as usual ... I wanted to warn you people ... but I came too late ... for the first time I feel weighed down, that my blood has weight. Finally I have weight. I'm heavy, I am ... heavy. A nice feeling. Winter will soon be over.

In Wenders' work, this really is the moment at which Vogler's role as the character Winter comes to an end, though he is raised from the dead once more a year later in *Lisbon Story*. It is the end of the story of Bruno Winter, who experienced the flow of time in an open-ended, episodic narrative structure, and a plot without highlights. In *Far Away, So Close*, however, he too has finally taken up a way of life befitting a star of a gangster movie: he is involved in a spying intrigue, takes photographs, and listens for the same criminal group that hires Cassiel. This activity kills him. In fact, time itself catches up with Winter too, and shoots him through the heart (the sound of a clock ticking can be heard in the background as Winter speaks). That he feels the proximity to death and his story as a weight mirrors Damiel's will in *Wings of Desire* to feel the weight of existence. Damiel's last action before he becomes human is to fondle the stone paperweight he had taken from Marion's caravan earlier, and tosses in his hands as if trying to feel its weight. Here, Damiel moves from one temporal dimension into another. In other words, in becoming a mortal human he, in a sense, dies at the same time. And as he dies he feels, finally, his existence as weight. Cassiel too tests his weight as soon as he stands in the (eastern) centre of Berlin, a human for the first time. And as he dies he hangs suspended from a circus trapeze device – a kind of elastic rope – between the earth and the space the angels occupy. Before he releases himself to fall to his death, Flesti's last word of advice is 'make yourself heavy. You have to use your dead weight.' The dead weight is the fact that, once the angel Cassiel becomes human he, like Damiel, knows that he has brought about his own death. Compared with his angelic existence, his time on earth will, anyway, seem just like a blink of the eye. His angelic last words as a human, in fact, are 'fucking gravity!' and his last act, to save the little girl, is at one and the same time the greatest confirmation of his life and a headlong rush into death. He only really lived if he takes this step, and dies. For Winter, the greatest satisfaction was to have a story that he could feel as a weight, and he feels this weight, this satisfaction, at the moment of his death. His and Cassiel's stories have their meaning and relevance defined by the death of their respective stories.

If life only becomes a story after death, which Wenders seems to assert through his hero, Friedrich Munroe, whose famous phrase, 'life goes by without the need to turn it into stories,' rings with irony when he is murdered at the end of *The State of Things*, then in leaving most of his narratives open, Wenders avoids it ever coming to the death of the narrative, and hence to the creation of a real story. If death is the 'sanction of everything the storyteller can tell' and if, as Walter Benjamin claims, the storyteller 'borrows his authority from death',[41] then Wenders denies that he is in the business of telling stories in images. A story is only a real story when it has an ending, Grob asserts,[42] and he goes on to quote Sartre's *Nausea*:

When you are living, nothing happens. The settings change, people come in and go out, that's all. There are never any beginnings. Days are tacked on to days without rhyme or reason, it is an endless, monotonous addition ... That's living. But when you tell about life, everything changes ... events take place one way and we recount them the opposite way. You appear to begin at the beginning: 'It was a fine autumn evening in 1922. I was a solicitor's clerk at Marommes.' And in fact you have begun at the end. It is there, invisible and present, and it is the end which gives these few words the pomp and value of a beginning ... And the story goes on in reverse: the moments have stopped piling up on one another in a happy-go-lucky manner, they are caught by the end of the story which attracts them and each of them in turn attracts the preceding moment.[43]

Or, as Pasolini describes it, cinema can reorder the events of a lifetime into a synthetic sequence of highlights that can then constitute a film. Again, Pasolini's emphasis is on how the death of a particular event can bring about its existence:

I must repeat here that a life, with all its stories, can only be fully and truly deciphered after death: then, its temporal dimension contracts and what is meaningless falls away ... At the very moment of death – after the intervention of montage – the continuum of life loses the whole endlessness of time ... After death, this continuity of life ceases to exist, but *its sense* is still there. ... Unlike in life, or in the cinema, in a film the meaning of an action ... is indeed defined by the meaning of the corresponding real action ... but its sense is already complete and can be deciphered, as if death had already set in. That means that in film, time is expired, even if it is fiction. So, one has to accept that one is forced to tell stories. Time is not that of life, as long as it lives, but that of time after death: as such, it is real, not an illusion, and it can easily be the time of a story in a film.[44]

On one hand, Wenders recognises that the practice of leaving a story relatively open at both ends weakens its similarity with traditional narrative forms, allowing it to extend its space. On the other, he realises the value of a conclusive end to stories for the meaning of the stories. Only *The State of Things*, which marks the end of the first leg of Wenders' journey, has an abrupt and dramatic ending. Though Kolker and Beicken consider Travis' tale in *Paris, Texas* to have a beginning, middle and end, he drives off into the desert having left his son with Jane.[45] For him, the story is not over yet, for this was just the first major step in his reintegration into society. In his experiments with drama, tension, and closure in *The American Friend*, *The State of Things* and *Far Away, So Close*, Wenders proved to himself, if nothing else, the validity of his thesis that 'stories are impossible, but it's impossible to live without them. That's the mess I'm in',[46] and that you cannot, in fact, rely on a story as he had speculated in *The State of Things*.

Not just *Far Away, So Close*, but all of Wenders' films condemn the traditional filmic narrative diegetically in that, whenever Wenders has allowed any of his characters to experience a story with a tight structure, a conclusive end, a psychologically motivated beginning and dramatic high-points, the character always dies at the end of the story he had begun to experience. The stories always lead to the inevitability of death under the unrelenting pressure of time's onward march. This condemnation simultaneously champions Wenders' alternative, so consistently applied and developed in each of his films except *The Scarlet Letter* and *Hammett*, which Wenders considers to be momentary lapses of judgement. This concept rests on an episodic narrative structure which promotes the uniqueness of all events that occur in the films, not just the highlights, enabling them to stand on their own, without necessarily leading to narrative conclusion. It is a tactic to lessen the potential for the uncontrollable filmic story to become over-important, to become more important than the films' images, the real document of the appearance of things. Story in Wenders' films is, and remains, little more than a necessary framework on which to hang the images.

But the impression of timelessness that characterises the episodes of a film such as *Kings of the Road* is raised because, in the absence of any specific goal or conclusion, the film has no obvious time-markers incorporated into the narrative. The treatment of time here rather reflects the experience of the journey: the characters eat, sleep, drive, rest, fight, even defecate on screen. Then the film is finished. In dominant cinema, time is ordinarily strictly controlled to assure narrative continuity, as described by Lewis Herman in *The Classical Hollywood Cinema*:

> Care must be taken that every hole is plugged; that every loose string is tied together; that every entrance and exit is fully motivated, and that they are not made for some obviously contrived reason; that every coincidence is sufficiently motivated to make it credible; that there is no conflict between what has gone on before, what is going on currently, and what will happen in the future; that there is complete consistency between present dialogue and past action – that no baffling question marks are left over at the end of the picture to detract from the audience's appreciation of it.[47]

One can generally state, then, that in films that have, from the beginning, the intention to bring a story to its end, every shot acts like a building block that at once adds information and moves the plot of the film onwards. Once the end of the story is reached, it is all that counts because every other unit that came before was placed in the film in order to reach this ending. Other functions of editing such as suture, special effects or suspense also have the ultimate goal of realising narrative impact on the spectator. In these cases, one can say that time has been manipulated because, through editing, each fragment of the film contributes to a synthetic scheme of the unfolding of events. From this point of view, one could also claim that every film is necessarily fiction because, through the editing process, it is a synthetic reconstruction of a reality that never in fact existed. Each unit, in the case of a film that has as its ultimate goal the telling of a story, is therefore placed in an artificial connection with other units. In themselves, though, they have no meaning other than in relation to other units. A degree of autonomy between units, however, can be a first step towards reducing the artificiality of a filmic narrative construction.

Clearly, Herman's guidelines leave no room for error. But neither do they leave any room for a film to speak of something other than the immediate concern of narrating a story. Though Wenders keeps an equally tight control over time and sequence in his films, he imposes a different set of regulations to do this. Rather than 'taking care that every hole is plugged', Wenders prefers, if the opportunity arises, to show the hole in its entirety, to present time as much as possible in its natural dimension. This is most obviously the case in Wenders' early films, with their long, uncut sequences, images of space that recall Wenders' description of himself when he painted as 'a painter of space engaged on a quest for time. It never occurred to me that this search should be called "storytelling".'[48]

Much less radical in his later films, Wenders made less and less use of such extremely long sequences, and he became more sure of cutting by the time of *Alice in the Cities*, when he began to realise that it is still possible to respect natural time and space even without simply switching on the camera and letting it run until the reel is finished. This is much more a question of the relation one shot has with the shots that precede and succeed it, than that a cut brings about the beginning and the end of a certain period of filmic time. Here again, the different cutting patterns in *Kings of the Road* and *Until the End of the World* show that, although cutting patterns may differ from film to film, Wenders tries, in these films, to treat time thematically, using editing to express the experience of the passage of time. The former film represents the most extreme case in Wenders' oeuvre of a free narrative development, since it was made for the most part without a script having been prepared, whilst the latter gives Filippo D'Angelo the impression that Wenders wanted to test his new-found trust in the power of stories, due to the tighter editing patterns and stronger story.[49] The border/hemisphere crossings in *Until the End of the World* are represented simply by inconspicuous cuts. Changes in location are not immediately obvious, even if they move the film from one side of the planet to the other. The gangster elements incorporated within this film additionally have the effect of speeding up the narrative development in the first half of the film.

During the preparations for the filming of *Kings of the Road*, conversely, Wenders drove the length of the East German/West German border several times. Consequently, the film documents his own journey in that the space between one place and the next is covered by road, and can be felt in the film. Both films are about the movements of the protagonists through a landscape, and their journey – the act of being on the move – becomes a main narrative thrust of the films. *Kings of the Road* is about Robert and Bruno's journey, and also about Wenders' journey through the same landscape. It is as if they are merely playing out his diary entries from the location scouting he did himself. Time is respected in *Until the End of the World* mainly because, through the invisible cuts between continents, Wenders expresses the impression that transport and communications, compared to the days of *Kings of the Road*, have become everyday, easier and quicker. The cuts thus respect the flow of time as he may have experienced it. Equally, the absence of such cuts in *Kings of the Road*, or rather, the focus on the act of moving itself, perhaps reflects Wenders' impression then that travel was something for which time had to be taken. In each case, narrative structure is episodic, and the points of contact between episodes – represented by a cut – strengthen the impression that we have witnessed a complete cycle of time – and of movement through space – and that the next cycle is about to begin. Each episode keeps its independent character in this way and, instead of serving to construct a synthetic time continuum in the form of a story, each episode is like a detail that is rounded off before the next begins. This is partly why so many of Wenders' films are road movies: the genre is suited to the fairly loose stringing together of units that are permitted a certain degree of autonomy, and that do not, therefore, serve exclusively to construct a story, but rather they aim to document the '*Lauf der Zeit*'.[50] Wenders minimalises plot to such an extent that it is often no more than a framework narrative that tells 'the story of the man who...'. This story has an episodic structure so that each episode is featured, rather than placing the emphasis on the conclusion of the story; usually, the conclusion, in the traditional sense, is even omitted. What remains is the bare outline of a story necessary for the presentation of images in the body of a film. This is how Wenders tries to bring his images to word, to allow them to speak, and is the basis of his aesthetic and of his concept of filmic storytelling.

Wenders' aesthetic of creative perception

A single photograph is unable to narrate a story because a story that is narrated can only develop over a period of time. Yet a photograph is a document of physical appearance, which is the only concrete information pertaining to the image that it can offer. This information is of an empirical nature. But that does not mean that the meaning of an image (a photograph or a filmic episode) is equal to the empirical content of the image, since the evidence of physical appearance offered by a photograph can be characterised by many other factors. One of these factors is that the image is always a record of appearance in the past, at a specific moment which the flow of time immediately and irrevocably overtakes. Whether or not the subject of the photograph changes in appearance is immaterial, but this aspect allows one, even forces one, to consider a photograph to have caught also a specific moment, a piece of time, as well as having

FIGURE 5 *Kings of the Road* (© 1976, Road Movies Filmproduktion GmbH)

documented the appearance of a specific physical space. A photograph is therefore something that belongs to history in the very (present) moment of its creation. The photograph speaks of history, and its viewer must accept its meaning as such. The historical meaning inherent to a photographic reproduction of reality is attached to it by virtue of the technical characteristics of the medium.

But photographic and filmic images also express a view of reality from the personal point of view of the photographer or director, who selects the time and space to be recorded and uses the reproductive qualities of the medium and montage – the art of juggling with time and space – to express this point of view. Even the images of *Silver City*, a film that suggests the complete withdrawal of the director and the absence of the filmic apparatus from the film-making process, document the appearance of physical reality only because the director selected the locations for filming. Though Wenders avoided the use of cuts in this film, each of the thirteen time-sequences is finite, beginning and ending in accordance with the director's choices. In empowering his images to speak with the authority of their empirical content, Wenders, as much as any other film-maker, is himself speaking through his images. The empirical evidence that the images present is a record that exists because of the perception and vision of the film-maker. The specificity of space and time represented in a photographic image means that, although it offers empirical evidence of physical appearance, reality has nevertheless been interpreted by the photographer/film-maker. This is, along with historical meaning, a second level of meaning that is attached to any photographic representation of reality.

In view of Wenders' concerns about the important role of images in establishing and retaining the identity of things, the manipulation of images for commercial and narrative purposes (the vampire narrative) and the inflation of images through television can be considered a destructive interpretation of reality because of the potential for a schism to develop between reality and depicted reality. One might consequently consider a mode of representation that preserves or even (re)establishes the natural link between image and reality/subject, which is Wenders' objective, as a creative interpretation of reality. The photographer's interpretation can be judged from the images he makes because, according to Wenders, the chosen *Einstellung* (shot) also says something about the photographer's *Einstellung* (attitude) towards reality. If this is so, then a photographer's/film-maker's mode of perception is decisive for determining the nature of his interpretation of the physical world. A mode of perception that is attentive to the unique identity of phenomena would therefore be conditional for a creative interpretation, in film images, of physical reality.

The act of seeing – observation and perception – is thematised in Wenders' films precisely because vision is one of the senses that contribute to the formation and understanding of identity. The discourse is held on two different levels: diegetically, through the drawing of contrasts between the perceptual habits of different characters in the films; and practically, in that the conclusions Wenders reaches through making these contrasts plain are reflected in the way the films are made. The glance Wenders' camera casts over the world therefore also betrays his attitude with regard to reality. His images, which must transmit most of the information in Wenders' films due to his consistent refusal to develop psychological storylines, nevertheless interpret the physical world. If the spectator receives the information transmitted in images, then he learns not only about the appearance of physical reality, but also about Wenders' attitude towards reality. This non-empirical information is, in the absence of story, how Wenders' films narrate.

In film, the image is the key by which we can gauge the perception of the director: the camera is his eye, and the image we see is his account of what he has seen. Wenders has likened the kind of vision he desires for his films to the vision of children, whom he considers to enjoy the purest perception.

In my films, children are present as the film's own fantasy, the eyes the film would like to see with. A view of the world that isn't opinionated, a purely

ontological gaze. And only children really have that gaze ... Like the little boy
at the end of *Kings of the Road*, sitting at the station, doing his homework. He's
actually my dream of a film director.[51]

The child figures in Wenders' films usually play an important part in guiding adult
figures who are too blinded by the abundance of images to notice things. Kolker and
Beicken consider the child figure to act as a point of certainty, whose innocence is
largely due to their ignorance of German history, but there are many children in
Wenders' films who have no link whatsoever with Germany yet perform a similar role.
Perhaps the child figures represent an innocence of perception in the more general
sense. Wenders' position is rather more in line with that of Norbert Grob, who
considers this breakdown in adult subjectivity as much more of a general affliction
connected to image-commercialisation and inflation as Wenders describes it:

> In the maelstrom of technically produced imaging systems and coding patterns,
> it is today the 'simple' images to which the hopes of a complex intellect are
> pinned: as if a 'simple life' could spring forth from 'simple images', and a pure
> disposition could be recoupable from pure observation.[52]

Alice, who helps Winter to restore his vision after his American experience, is only the
first, but the most important example of this aspect of children's vision in Wenders'
films. The boy at the end of *Kings of the Road* describes what he sees and writes his
observations in a school book. 'It's that easy?' Robert asks the boy. 'It's that easy!' is
the reply. What Robert glimpses here is the possibility of seeing without requiring an
understanding beyond the fact of the existence of the things seen: simply remaining
open to visual stimulation, to ordinary phenomena. For Wenders, such perception
raises the potential, in film, for truth in a representation of physical reality:

> The great thing about seeing for me is what distinguishes it from thinking,
> namely that it doesn't entail having an opinion ... In seeing you can come to a
> view of another person, an object, the world, that doesn't imply an opinion ...
> I like the word insight. It suggests you can have truth and understanding just
> from seeing ... For me, seeing is immersing myself in the world.[53]

Wenders' films attempt to reproduce this mode of perception by emphasising the
act of observation and drawing the spectator into active participation, making him
take part in a search. The activity of searching out images that tell a story from the

given environment is common to all of Wenders' films, but particularly in the road movies, the constant movement of the characters and with them the director and the camera, adds a new dimension to the activity of observation. The fact of moving on and arriving in a place that had previously been unknown to a character, even to the director, as in the case of Tokyo in the film *Tokyo Ga*, means that finding is at the same time a constantly necessary and renewed activity. It would be possible to make a road movie without casting an eye on the surroundings, without giving up a strictly structured and prescribed story, but this would defeat the object of movement: the movement would be extraneous to the film and its story. But in Wenders' road movies, the act of seeing, when combined with constant motion through cities and landscapes, even necessitates the act of discovering. Constant motion means constantly renewing images that have to be examined, searched, before they can be properly perceived.

The shots for which Wenders is probably best known in his road movies are through the window of a moving vehicle. It is important that the conditions of movement are made clear because, as the vehicle is made obvious, the shots are presented as the vision of one of the characters: a subjective point of view on the landscapes. Consequently, the characters and the audience are drawn into the act of moving and of film-viewing respectively, as a searching activity. What Grob terms a 'panoramistic' shot is thus characterised by the potentially endlessly changing image.[54] Compared to a pan, which is limited to observing the 360 degrees of space around the camera, the panoramistic shot characteristic of Wenders' road movies promotes the searching/observing activity because there are no real limits at which the shots must stop, which imitates biological vision. The only thing that changes in the image is the image itself, hence, this must be watched closely. The audience follows the camera, which follows the characters who often just look at the landscape passing by through the window. Landscapes and details raise questions in the minds of the spectator, thus drawing attention back to the details to find more evidence. For the spectator, this search for evidence in the details is an act of personal discovery, giving the impression that the details must exist apart from the films' stories, that they are also witnessing a documentation of spaces. Wenders makes the reasons behind this kind of film-making practice plain: answering to the charge that his characters and his films seem to have aimless narrative trajectories, he explains:

> You're right, they're not going anywhere; or rather, it's not important for them
> to arrive anywhere particular. What's important is having the right 'attitude',
> to be moving. That's their aim: to be on the road. I'm like that myself too; I

prefer 'travelling' to 'arriving'. The condition of motion is very important to me. If I've been too long in a place, I somehow get uncomfortable; I'm not saying I get bored, but I get the feeling I'm less open to stimuli than when I'm moving. The best way I've found of making films is moving on – my imagination works best under that condition. As soon as I've been too long in a place I can't think of any fresh images, I'm no longer free.[55]

But reproducing the simplicity of a child's vision encourages and demands visual agility and dexterity of the spectator, who is drawn into the act of searching by the absence of psychological explanation. To be just shown things means, on the one hand, that the audience is to some extent left to come to its own conclusions about what it sees, and on the other, that the director who shows is able to direct attention at particular things in various different ways, depending on how the film equipment is employed. These are the narrative strategies the director has at hand and can use in order to transmit his interpretation of the physical world by abstracting the empirical information the film images offer.

That this kind of narration in images has to do with abstracting reality is reflected by those critics who have made attempts at defining or describing the nature of the information it transmits in equally abstract terms. In Kracauer's formulation, prolonged observation is the key to arriving at abstract information based in documentary images.[56] Quoting Alfred North Whitehead's *Science and the Modern World* (1925), Kracauer suggests that this kind of observation, though desirable, must be learned:

When you understand all about the sun, and all about the atmosphere and all about the rotation of the earth, you may still miss the radiance of the sunset. There is no substitute for the direct perception of the concrete achievement of a thing in its actuality. We want concrete facts with a highlight thrown on what is relevant to its preciousness ... What I mean is art and aesthetic education. It is, however, art in such a general sense that I hardly like to call it by that name. Art is a special example, what we want is to draw out habits of aesthetic apprehension.[57]

Like Kracauer, Norbert Grob emphasises the desire for a perception capable of penetrating through the visible surface of physical reality to discern the 'preciousness' of objects. Though he considers film, particularly Wenders' cinema, the art-form that is most suited to this objective, he too defines the product of such filmic perception in abstract terms, always coming to the conclusion that it has the character of something secretive:

> In his early writings, Balázs speaks of 'the living physiognomy that all things have' and about how there is 'no art that is so destined to show this face of objects as film. Because film not only shows the single, rigid physiognomy of things, but also its secretive facial expressions.' Wenders dedicates himself to this game; he allows his films the time to concentrate on the face of things.[58]

The hidden secrets borne by objects and images have occupied Wenders since *Kings of the Road* up until his most recent films. In *Beyond the Clouds*, he appears confident in the belief that even the filmic medium will never manage to reach so far beneath the surface appearance of things, that no one will ever see the true reality behind the surface image. Through the figure of the Director (John Malkovich), Wenders quotes a well-known dictum of Antonioni from 1964:

> We know that behind each image there is another image that is closer to reality, and behind that another even purer than the one before, and behind that image yet another image, and so on, until you reach the last, absolute image that no one will ever be able to see.

But, as Wenders confesses in *The Logic of Images*, he finds it more important to have the right *Einstellung* (attitude) than to arrive at some destination.[59] Perhaps he also finds it worth remaining open to the visual world, promoting a creative kind of perception, even though the absolute and true image of reality may prove to be beyond the reach of the cinema, or remain an indefinable abstract quality (leaving the spectator to decide what constitutes absolute truth in an image). Wenders desires an articulate cinematic image that both imitates natural perception, remaining open to all phenomena, and is also able to allow things to present and represent themselves. In this way, his cinema is based on the image as the primary information-bearing device. Narrative development, restricted to the role of a framework in which to present the images, is abated through the open-ended episodic form as well as a low degree of psychological explanation and motivation. Wenders attempts to make reality itself transparent, to bring the secret within things to the surface of the image, and hopes that, through careful observation, the spectator may catch a glimpse of the uniqueness of existence. This is a purely phenomenological approach to film-making.

CHAPTER THREE

commentaries

The following examination of Wim Wenders' work in the context of his position on the film image and its relation to narrative seeks to take into account the notable diversity of his extraordinarily prolific filmic output. The films selected therefore respect the fact that, while the feature films are, generally speaking, most suited to demonstrate the image/story problematic, the documentaries also merit particular consideration because they are extremely valuable as personal essays on images and image-making.

Each film analysed in this chapter emphasises different aspects of Wenders' exploration. Of the feature films, *Alice in the Cities* best exhibits the tendency in Wenders' films for the foregrounding of observational activity – the act of seeing. This is also the only road movie discussed in this examination. *Paris, Texas* and *Wings of Desire* focus more on the search for a form, a narrative structure to allow the images to retain their semantic force as a way of preserving the identity of their subjects, which are lost through image manipulation. In the diary film *Tokyo Ga*, Wenders goes in search of the Tokyo of Yazujiro Ozu's films, but finds modern-day Tokyo does not divulge to him anything of Ozu's city, which seems only to have been preserved in images. Wenders' latest feature, *The Million Dollar Hotel*, is, from the point of view of its structure, the complete opposite of a road movie, being set exclusively within the confines of a Los Angeles hotel and its immediate vicinity. Here, American television, and commercialised images in general, are portrayed as degrading the stories of the lives of the film's protagonists to the level of sensationalistic and seductive entertainment material presented as news items. The victims, it seems, are expelled to live an existence on the edges of society. Lastly, a section has also been devoted to the film *Lisbon Story*, in which, through the sound technician Philip Winter, Wenders suggests that sound in film can play a similar role to the image, to allow things to be seen differently.

Alice in the Cities

Being his first independent production (both the previous films produced after Wenders' graduation from film school were made for television stations), *Alice in the Cities* is the film in which Wenders was first able to freely put his personal film aesthetic or language to the test. It is a road movie that features an extremely economic use of plot and a linear, open, episodic narrative structure. Beginning in the US, the film thematically contrasts two different modes of vision: that of a child, Alice, and that of a travelling journalist, Philip Winter, who, like his creator, seems to be testing a media-induced impression of the US: 'the land of images'.

Alice in the Cities begins towards the end of a pre-history to the film, the untold story of Philip Winter's journey through America which, to a certain extent, determines the unfolding of the story we are about to witness. The establishing sequence is less an introduction to the film than a beginning of something, and explains what the film is about. The first shot of the film, a pan on an aircraft in flight, past an American street sign for B-67th Street, ending on a shot of an empty beach, establishes the geographical location at which the film's story begins, but which is situated midway through Winter's journey through America. In the third shot we see Winter make a Polaroid photograph of the beach. He is alone, leaning against a pier. Winter compares his Polaroid against the actual object, a wooden construction on the beach, then begins to sing a song that would have been familiar to the audience in the mid-1970s: 'Under the boardwalk / down by the sea / on a blanket with my baby / that's where I wanna be.' Just as he seems to compare his Polaroid images with reality, Winter also seems to be testing an impression of America, gained from the popular culture of the day, against reality. Everything seems in place, but Winter is alone, there is no sign of any 'baby' beside him and Winter seems to have resigned himself to this state of affairs. This song, and the Polaroid photographs Winter makes, outline the nature of the film's exploration: the possible consequences of visual over-stimulation, and the relationship between images and reality.

The American setting for the first half of *Alice in the Cities* is highly relevant: American films and Hollywood have been the strongest influence on Wenders' film-making, which is evidenced in his adaptation of essentially American genres such as the road movie here, film noir in *The State of Things*, *The Goalkeeper's Fear of the Penalty Kick*, *The American Friend*, the western genre in *Kings of the Road* and *Paris, Texas*. But this is also the film in which Wenders begins to relativise his idealistic picture of America as 'the land of free vision'.[1] Beginning to question the validity of the 'American Dream', exported to all parts of the world through the successful export of American musical and cinematic culture worldwide, Wenders here uses his film to announce the death of the mythical American cinema of the 1940s and 1950s that had so inspired him, finding one reason for its extinction in the kind of vision and visuality nurtured by the television phenomenon and the commercial interests it represents. The television set that Winter later destroys in his hotel room is showing a film by John Ford, *Young Mr. Lincoln*, when the film is interrupted by television advertising. That is the point at which Winter gets up from his bed and knocks the television set from its table, suggesting that television, rather than the film itself provokes the unusually aggressive outburst in the normally composed Winter. The last sequence of *Alice in the Cities* completes the picture when we see the headline announcing Ford's death in a newspaper Winter is reading. The associations made in the introductory sequence, the final sequence and in the motel sequence when Winter smashes the television set are complex, but fully consistent with Wenders' belief that it is above all the introduction

FIGURE 6 *Alice in the Cities* (© 1974, Road Movies Filmproduktion GmbH)

of television and the resulting inflation of commercialised images that brought about the demise of the mythical American cinema that was such an inspiration to him and many other film-makers of his generation.

The lost dream of American cinema is, for Wenders, present in American music: 'One should be able to make films about America that are only made of long shots' are the first words said by Wenders in his short film *3 American LPs*. 'That already exists in music, in American music.' This is followed by a shot from a high balcony in the Munich suburbs showing the empty landscape miles into the distance, which is held for almost ninety seconds. Wenders elaborates on the notion of films consisting entirely of panoramic shots in his 1970 article on Ford, 'Emotion Pictures: Slowly Rockin' on'. Whilst expressing his disapproval at most contemporary films here – 'pictures that block off your vision' – he describes what he misses about Ford's cinema:

> I miss the friendliness, the care, the thoroughness, the seriousness, the peace, the humanity of John Ford's films; I miss those faces that are never forced into anything; those landscapes that aren't just backgrounds ... Music from America is more and more replacing the sensuality that the films have lost: the merging of blues and rock and country music has produced something that can no longer be experienced only with the ears, but which is visible, and forms images, in space and time. This music is above all the music of the American West, whose conquest is the subject of John Ford's films ... San Francisco and Los Angeles also gave birth to the American cinema. Meanwhile, 'Motion Pictures' has become a definition of music. [2]

Wenders' character, Philip Winter, would like to believe in the promised dream, but finds that it is empty in a land where images have pervaded every aspect of life, to the extent that he, in a sense, becomes blinded by them. With the announcement of Ford's death at the end of the film, the camera rises from the train that is taking Alice and Winter to Munich until it is high enough for a panoramistic shot of the whole of the surrounding landscape up to the horizon that fills the frame. Wenders sought to give the impression of seeing all Germany in this shot, wanted to fly as high as possible.[3] After the forests of signposts, urban and suburban streets and the psychological numbness of the American city and landscapes, Germany – Europe – appears like a clean sheet of paper, an emptiness soothing to the eye, an as yet undiscovered land that offers the willing eye the opportunity and the invitation to explore, discover, and perhaps even find a new story. This last sequence exhibits the type of panoramic shot that Wenders praises in Ford's films, that he considers to be present only in contemporary American music. It is but a dream of America, a land where the visible has become so predominant that it leads to blindness.

The first sequences of *Alice in the Cities* feature a mixture of narrative techniques, both conventional and unconventional. The physical space is established in an establishing shot, yet it introduces the beginning of the long road that the film will take as it progresses towards the end of a journey, rather than a space in which the narrative will unfold. We are introduced to the main protagonist, Philip Winter, and immediately gain some knowledge about his psychological state through the emptiness around him, and his melancholy behaviour. The human figure initially appears no more important than the empty backgrounds, creating a near complete homology between the individual figure and the world of objects that he photographs. Through the lines of the song Winter sings to himself, the soundtrack simultaneously provides information similar to the information we gain from the film's images, about the absence of a longed-for warmth of togetherness. In this example of image/sound reversal, the words Winter sings yield the same information as the images of the film: a man, under a boardwalk, by the sea. Both image and sound also inform us of the figure's loneliness, the absence in reality of the dream of being 'on a blanket with my baby / that's where I wanna be'.

Audience identification is encouraged through familiarity with the song Winter sings, but also through conventional suture. The film begins with a subjective shot of an aircraft flying above, then an objective/independent shot of Winter sitting on the beach, who is in turn looking at the photographs he has made, then more subjective point-of-view shots as he compares the photographs with the reality before him. These cutting patterns immediately involve the spectator in a game of looking, comparing and looking again, aligning audience point-of-view with Winter's, at the same time as introducing the film's theme of observation. All but one of the images that come before the point at which Winter leaves the beach is either a shot on the figure or a subjective shot representing what the figure sees. Whilst there is no apparent story structure in this establishing sequence, the audience gains an understanding mainly through what they are shown, or through what they hear.

As Wenders continues to mix conventional with non-conventional narrative techniques over the part of *Alice in the Cities* covering Winter's drive to New York City, the emphasis on sound and image-based narration remains constant, which lends the film a documentary quality. The movement of Winter's car is presented in a mixture of different shots: tracking, then an objective shot of Winter in the car, followed by a subjective shot as the car approaches the beach a second time. Later, pans are also used to follow the movement of the car. The passage of time and distance is represented, quite conventionally, by a cut-in/fade-out sequence, in which the changing weather also gives a sense of an expanded passage of time through space over the progress of this road movie.

This progress is punctuated every time Winter stops to take a photograph of objects or locations he finds along the roadside: a different part of the beach where there are more people, a tower with the words 'Surf City'. Already in this first part of the road that will lead Winter back to Germany, these roadside attractions provide evidence of the phenomenological approach to film which Wenders pursues. The combination of images of the open road – which, in this case, seems clustered by signs, lampposts and telegraph poles when compared with the sense of freedom the road represents in one of Wenders' favourite films, *Easy Rider* – and the inquisitive camera that focuses attention on the immediate environment along the stretch of the road at the beginning of this film, is familiar from Wenders' earlier work, most particularly *Summer in the City*. It, too, is largely a collection of filmic observations from a moving car. Here, the sense of the pictures Winter makes does not seem to contribute in any way to the development of a plot until New York is reached, where Winter explains to the agent of the publication for which he is supposed to be writing an article why he has only accumulated a mountain of photographs, but has no written material to deliver. Here, Wenders and Winter are, essentially, doing the same work – documenting the appearance of a certain location at a certain time.

The road and the motor vehicle are Wenders' ideal mode of transport for the task of documenting physical reality in moving images (this might also have been the least costly option for his first independent production). The camera follows Winter's gaze through the windows of the car. It brings us close to the 'Surf City' tower in an extreme close-up, which recalls the drive through Antonioni's Los Angeles at the beginning of *Zabriskie Point*, and which has the effect of isolating the image from the already very slender form of a narrative even while the car is in motion, the story getting under way. At the beach, the camera is mounted on the bonnet of the car. We only hear that Winter takes a picture – we are familiar with the sound of the then new Polaroid camera from the film's opening sequence – while the camera shows independently the scene that he photographs. And when Winter pulls into a roadside cafeteria to look through his collection of images, we see the director put on a record on the jukebox in the background as if to state that the journey so far was also his journey, that they are his images, his documentation of the American South-West in the mid-1970s. What more evidence could be necessary to make the statement that the intention of this part of the film has been a filmic documentation of the appearance of physical reality, other than the presence in one of those images of the master photographer himself: almost like a snap-shot of a tourist passing through, proof that this is not just some invented story, but one based on personal experience.

Drawing from Wenders' poem 'The American Dream', his account of his first experiences of the US, it seems clear that he has largely transferred his sentiments onto his character: Wenders writes about how he perceives America as a land where one is so surrounded by advertising images that vision becomes eroded. Winter expresses a similar sentiment when, after arriving in New York, he excuses his inability to write, reasoning that 'the story is about things you can see'. Instead of preparing a written document describing his experiences travelling through America, Winter has produced something like a photo-reportage. He has abandoned the arbitrary mediation of the word – writing – in favour of the immediacy and the comparative concreteness of the photographic image, more suited to reclaiming the predominantly visible aspects of contemporary American society.

Compared with the distortions of the verbal language, photographs reproduce reality without altering its form. Photographs show the many-sidedness of what a word catches in one term and, on the contrary, they also catch objects in single images for which many words would be necessary to describe. Winter seems to be attempting to slow down the torrent of constantly changing images that permeate life in the US, to catch a moment in the very process of turning into something else before it disappears forever. Yet, despite the fact that Winter photographs the things that interest him – an attempt to isolate the objects of interest in images that concretise the appearance of reality in one visual representation – he still cannot bring himself to express the meaning of his experiences in words. From the photographs he makes, and his reaction when they have developed, it is clear that Winter is indeed hoping to express something in abstract terms, some meaning attached to the objects and landscapes he photographs, which the concrete representations in the photographs do not seem to permit.

The first image of the empty beach is a contemplative, carefully composed representation – an abstraction of Winter's inner state. The emptiness seems to disturb Winter, and he drives to another part of the same beach where there are some people playing ball games to make a second photograph, one that fits in with the overall impression of an otherwise visually overloaded environment, but that denies his subjective experience of the moment that the first photograph represents. The contrast between these two images shows how Winter has become so distanced from the environment that he is no longer sure whether his own perception of the world around him reflects reality, or whether the camera's eye, and the concrete images it produces, is the true representation. This is a conflict between Winter's personal artistic intention (romantic contemplation and reflection), which also suggests the existence of an inner longing for peaceful images, and the negation of personal intent for other interests (Winter is also meant to be working). And the fact that Winter cannot decide which of these approaches is the more relevant – the image that fits in with his impressions, or the image that seems more relevant from the point of view of completing his assignment – is a symptom of the illness of images that Winter describes later, and which Wenders describes in similar terms in 'The American Dream'.

Winter is blinded and bewildered by the dominance of the visual aspect in his experience of America. This dominance is augmented by the abundance of images used for commercial purposes. Not only does Wenders consider the danger to exist of new, foreign meanings becoming attached to images through their use in advertising, meanings that are unrelated to the objects represented, but that these saturate the general visual aspect to the extent that fixed impressions are replaced by constantly changing ones, and objects no longer keep their unchangeable, final, recognisable visual identity. The speed of change allows no time for contemplation and reflection.

Winter seems to be trying to hold up the constantly changing visual aspect of things with the Polaroid photographs he makes. Filippo D'Angelo likens Polaroid technology (Winter's model of the Land Camera was an innovation of the 1940s), which differs from conventional photography in that there is no negative from which to make copies of the image, to an older art form, painting, asserting that the absence of a negative in Polaroid photography from which to make copies serves to 'recoup the "aura" of painting, lost in the age of technical reproducibility'.[4]

The 'aura' in painting that D'Angelo speaks of lies partly in the uniqueness of the original, partly in the act of freezing time, the catching of a moment before it has time to change, before things move on, not just because faithful copies of paintings could not easily be made before the development and industrialisation of copying and printing techniques. According to D'Angelo, Polaroid photographs, as opposed to conventional photography, offer a potential for the very same aura attached to painting: each is a unique representation of things, a single expression that cannot be repeated.

But D'Angelo is also referring to the creativity involved in painting, as well as the physical qualities that distinguish it and Polaroid photography. The act of slowing down the course of events, of freezing the momentary appearance of physical reality in the fixed frame of an image, is the nature of any visual medium whether it is based on still or moving images. This feature allows time for the contemplation and reflection necessary for the expression of the artist's interpretation of the given reality (the expression in the reproduction of innermost emotions; the relevance of the painting or its subject for the artist), which goes into the production of a painting, and which gives a painting its value (a value that becomes diminished if the same work is reproduced in large numbers, or is diffused as a reproduction). Norbert Grob draws on a phrase of the German painter Caspar David Friedrich, to whom Wenders alludes in *Wrong Movement* and *Until the End of the World*, to illustrate the importance of an artist's subjectivity in a representation of reality: 'A painter shouldn't just paint what he sees before him, but also what he sees within himself. If he sees nothing within himself, then he should refrain from painting what he sees before him.'[5]

Winter's snapshots represent such an attempt at holding up time before it has passed, to allow a moment's contemplation and still observation. His Polaroid camera offers him the same expressive potential as D'Angelo observes in painting, but he is nevertheless unable to find a relation, to develop a personal angle to all that he sees. Winter complains that 'it's never the same as it looked' when, having stopped at a service station to make a photograph of the station, a boy, who had been standing in front of the station, is not on the picture when it develops. As an illustration of how things can change before you have time to look again, this is a relatively crude example: the boy literally does not appear in the image. But Wenders makes the point that Winter is always looking in his photographs for the expression of something he sees, or perceives, and is disappointed when the image does not reflect or express the atmosphere that he had hoped to catch – an abstraction of reality, an emotion. The assumption is that, for Winter, it is too late, or, as he himself explains, the bombardment by images during his travels in America, particularly through television, which he admits to having watched every night (Winter claims to be so affected that things begin to look the same wherever he goes) has blinded him to the extent that he cannot develop a personal relation to the environment. He no longer sees anything within himself, and so accumulates a collection of images of 'what he sees before him'. His power of expression has become diminished because of the domination of the visual aspect that constantly feeds him new information: an overwhelming flood which threatens to drag Winter along.

There are two scenes in *Alice in the Cities* which feature direct attacks on television, and which show that this device lies at least partly at the root of Winter's problems with perception. The first night since the beginning of the film Winter spends in a roadside motel where he turns on the television. He begins to watch Ford's *Young Mr. Lincoln* before lying down on the bed and falling asleep. That Ford is one of the directors whom Wenders most admired at the time seems to dispute the suggestion that Winter serves as a kind of alter ego for Wenders, as he promptly turns away from the television

FIGURE 7 *Alice in the Cities* (© 1974, Road Movies Filmproduktion GmbH)

to sleep. In the following montage sequence, one of the few instances in Wenders' films where editing is used for expressive purposes, the television set appears against a backdrop of the window frame in which flashing advertising lights are framed. The television flickers into life and we see the first images of Ford's film before the image fades away in an eruption of static interference, which expresses the unsuitability of the televisual medium for cinematic films. The next time we see the television set the film is interrupted by a series of advertisements. We hear the words 'a mind is a terrible thing to waste: give to the United Negro College Fund' and the beginning of the next advertisement, apparently for tourism in Florida, at which point Winter gets up from the bed to smash the television set. The backdrop of neon advertising lights reinforces the theme of television as 'optical toxin'[6] as both emit a flickering light and through the suggestion of mind-poisoning in the text of the advertisement. This sequence is interrupted only by images of the sleeping Winter and a few seconds of his dream: images of an open road, emptiness. In America, at least, the reality – the view in the background through the window – sadly corresponds to the evidence for the commercialisation of film images in television, and the peace Winter is searching for to be able to 'see', to be able, that is, to translate his visual experience of America into words, only seems possible in his dreams.

The significance of this sequence is the filmic expression and statement of Wenders' theories that television contributed to the degradation of the former mythical American cinematic tradition, represented by the reference to Ford through the film *Young Mr. Lincoln*, through its appropriation of this tradition for its own commercial gain, before it had itself come of age as a visual language. The small, crackly image testifies to television's unsuitability for the broadcasting of cinematic films, whilst the interruption of the film for advertising illustrates the mechanisms by which film images are appropriated for commercial gain, threatening the fracturing of image and meaning.

Winter puts precisely this idea into words in the second instance of a direct attack on television in this film, when he is in a New York hotel room, taking notes while watching television:

> American television is inhuman not because it's all hacked up with commercials, though that's bad enough, but because, in the end, all programmes become commercials. Commercials for the status quo. Every image radiates the same disgusting, sickening message, a kind of boastful contempt. Every image wants something from you.

Here, again, as Winter watches television and writes his notes, the image is split: one half shows the television in close-up, the other half, the sleeping Alice in the background. Not only is television associated in both of these cases with 'inhumanity' (the television is framed against a backdrop of advertising signs in the former sequence) and with dreams (there are altogether three instances in which sleeping and dreaming are associated with television), but Alice, in the second instance, is a picture of peace and tranquillity and appears for the first time in the film as a possible guiding light for Winter to recover his vision. It will be Alice, after all, who leads Winter back to the relative visual peace of the German Rhineland and Ruhr regions, where he begins a search not for casual impressions, but for the stations marking Alice's real story.

But even Alice is threatened by the 'monstrosity' of television. The dream she describes in the Amsterdam hotel room later, in which she is bound to a chair in front of a television set and forced to watch a horror film, seals the association of television with a nightmarish concept, and makes plain the threat that Wenders perceives television to present for the purity, calmness and transparity of vision promised by cinema in its early days.

The New York sequence of *Alice in the Cities* serves primarily to introduce the figure of Alice and to further elaborate on Winter's problems with vision and Alice's possible role in helping him to see and comprehend things more clearly. Winter first meets Alice at New York's Pan Am office where he and Alice's mother (Lisa van Damm) both hope to obtain tickets for a flight to Germany. Winter and Lisa agree to find a hotel room together when they are told that they can only travel the next day. In the morning, the mother has disappeared, and instead of meeting her later as planned, Winter finds a note asking him to accompany Alice to Amsterdam where she would reach them the next day.

Unused to the company of a child, Winter takes Alice to the observation level in the Empire State Building in New York. Winter is impatient while Alice observes the city below through a pay-telescope. The camera assumes her point of view. For a moment, Winter and the story are completely forgotten, and the sequence becomes one of pure contemplation for its own sake. By chance a bird flies into the frame, and the camera follows it until it becomes lost in the jungle of Manhattan's sky-scrapers below. We, the spectators, see the first images of release and escape from the inner toils of the hero, Winter, since the beginning of the film – and it is significant that these images are presented as the vision of a child, Alice. From the composition of this sequence, it is clear that the bird flies into the frame quite by chance: the camera had previously been tracking along a different line but, once the bird enters the frame, the camera follows its path. This signals a desire in Wenders for the camera to enjoy the same openness of vision and attention that Alice – the first of a number of children who, in Wenders' films, are blessed with clear vision – shows for the incidental. Objects on the edge of the diegesis – here, the bird – are often allowed to drift into the frame, even though they may have little or no relevance for the development of the plot, as is the case here.

This evaluation of the cinema as an instrument capable of catching unique moments, such as the flight of a bird through Manhattan, seems like it has more to do with some magical property than with plain physical reality. But such coincidences are the fabric of everyday reality; the question is whether one notices them. Wenders explains that, for him, this is where the charm of the cinema is based:

> For me, the fun of telling stories and walking through the streets, into an apartment or in a train with a camera, is that something can happen that one didn't know about before, or something can appear that you didn't expect to appear.[7]

Secondly, the sequence shows the activity of making reality transparent through simple observation. Alice may just see the bird but, more importantly, the reproduction or interpretation of Alice's vision in the framing shows something about how this type of habitual vision might also offer the spectator a glimpse of some underlying reality, to make reality transparent. In watching the bird, we are shown how free it seems in comparison with the prison-like jungle of the city below, with its straight lines and sharp edges, its rows of windows that block a free vision.

From the point of view of narration – of finding Alice's mother or a home where she can be delivered – this scene has nothing at all to say. Neither does it have any relation, in the sense of building up meaning, with the shots that come before and after it. It is an entirely self-sufficient shot that has its own meaning defined simply by the occurrence of a bird flying between the skyscrapers of Manhattan. Time and space are respected in their real dimensions here because the image merely shows what it contains and is un-cut; it has no narrative relation to any other shot in the film, and therefore does not attempt to construct a narrative coherence of any sort. The only time that is relevant here is the time it takes for the bird to fly through the image, until it is out of sight. The space that this shot represents is in reality the space through which the bird flies in this time. The shot does not claim to be anything other than the documentation of this event, at this time and in this space. The objective of the shot is that the spectator sees what the camera records. It is a self-sufficient unit in that we do not stop to wonder whether the fact of the bird's presence will be decisive in the outcome of the story; the only importance of this sequence is that it occurred, has come to an end, but has been chosen for preservation by a film-maker who 'liked' it, and whose concern it is to capture something of his era: 'I always got my energy from wanting to capture something valid of the time in which I live.'[8]

In the section of *Alice in the Cities* covering Winter's and Alice's journey together from New York to Amsterdam, Wenders further diminishes the presence of any kind of recognisable narration in the conventional sense to the point that there is as good as no plot development from the moment the two protagonists leave New York for the airport, until they return to Amsterdam airport two days later to meet Alice's mother, who is expected to arrive. The narrative information one can speak of in this section – though this does not mean storytelling, rather, perhaps, characterisation – is what Winter and Alice do and say whilst they are in the process of waiting. Before the flight, Alice explores the airport, sits down to watch television and begins eating a sandwich. Winter presumably remains in his seat until he searches for and finds Alice, though, in the absence of parallel editing, this is not shown. During the flight, both characters sleep and eat, Winter makes a photograph and tries to write something in the toilet. Winter asks the stewardess for an aspirin. He and Alice play a word game. In Amsterdam, they go to the nearest hotel and fall asleep. The next day, they embark on a city tour, Winter has his hair cut and they return to the hotel to sleep. Twenty minutes – almost a fifth of the film – go by in this 'dead' period from when they leave New York until they discover that Alice's mother has not arrived in Amsterdam, which is the point at which the search for the grandmother begins, and the plot again assumes some relevance as far as the story is concerned. If one includes the seventeen minutes of 'dead' narrative time that go by from the film's beginning until Winter's arrival in New York's Pan Am office, then from the point of view of plot development, two-thirds of the film so far (until the fifty-fifth minute) describe the process of waiting or of moving, whilst the remaining eighteen minutes of this part of the film are used to introduce us to Alice and her mother (this is the only time Alice's mother appears in the film). With this barest outline of a story, it is clear that the relevance of the first half of *Alice in the Cities* lies almost entirely in the characterisation of the protagonists and in the images the continuously moving camera records. It is, furthermore, impossible to speak of any narrative peaks or dramatisation, since everything that has so far come into view of the camera has been simply revealed without any narrative importance attached to it. Their existence has been confirmed, but these objects disappear again for the remainder of the film unless they are in some way attached to one of the characters.

The line the film is following is thus a linear trajectory that never crosses its own path and never doubles back on itself. Both photographers, Winter and (the very present) Wenders, are travelling along this line, making visual records of the existence of the phenomena visible in a radius from the axis of the line to the horizon whilst they move onwards along the line, marked, presumably, on Wenders' road map – the basis for advancement in *Alice in the Cities*, just as in many of the other films. The end of the story is determined by the length of this line, rather than by dramatic fulfilment or conclusion, and here, as usual, the line continues beyond the end of the film. If the story has no obvious beginning or ending, one can speak of an imaginary infinite narrative line that continues beyond the film's 110-minute length. 'Story' is a result of movement over this time, the product of a development that depends on spatial and temporal logic, not on narrative intent. The story we witness is thus – as Wenders admits by leaving his narratives open at both ends – only a relatively insignificant part, a fragment of a larger story, which is the advancement of time and the existence of space. The camera is unable to record all existence and cannot be left to run infinitely, but the time recorded in *Alice in the Cities* is marked apart for the simple fact that it has been preserved in the form of a film.

Over the expanse of time it takes for the film and its main protagonists to move from New York to Amsterdam airport, the information the film offers us serves to further develop the characters and to continue the discourse that began in the first frames, rather than to develop a story. With Philip Winter already characterised as a European far from home, and so bewildered by the mass of visual information America has to offer that he is blinded, and with Alice having been presented as a possible cure for this blindness, Wenders begins to create a palpable tension between Alice and the main cause of Winter's blindness: television.

Just as Filippo D'Angelo forges a link between the spectator in *The American Friend* (represented by Jonathan Zimmerman, who is seduced into involvement in a story that seems to come straight from a Hollywood film), fascinated by, and culturally dependent on American cinematic culture (represented by the figure of Ripley), he makes a similar parallel between Alice, representative of early cinema by virtue of the purity of her vision, and Winter, for whom Alice would seem to promise a cure.

> Alice is the cinema by virtue of her way of seeing: Philip finds his identity in her because, unlike photography, cinema can reproduce movement. It is able to show Man in his spatial and temporal dimension, which photographs cannot. Man's infancy is like a return to the spontaneous creative energy, the ingenuity of an uncontaminated vision. The infancy of cinema is like a recouping of the descriptive purity of the 'evidence' of the representation.[9]

Wenders once again links television with dreams in the expression of this parallel. When, during the flight from New York to Amsterdam, Winter and Alice play a word game – Alice has to guess the letters that make up a word thought up by Winter – Alice exclaims that the word chosen by Winter, *Traum* (dream), should be disallowed: 'Only things that exist,' she says. This apparent reference to Winter's dream of calmness and emptiness during the television showing of Ford's *Young Mr. Lincoln*, interrupted by the television advertising slot, and Alice's suggestion that a corresponding reality does not exist, is a confirmation of Winter's distanced and idealistic picture of the reality of life in America – also expressed in the words of the song he sings at the very beginning of the film. Alice, conversely, does not believe what she cannot see or touch: here, she does not believe in a dream; in New York, she is not fooled when Winter pretends to blow out the lights illuminating the Empire State Building – on the stroke of midnight. She exhibits a much closer contact to the world than Winter; it is palpable to her. Winter cannot have his dream, despite his conviction that there is an underlying harmony behind the distracting visual facades in America.

Alice's quasi-psychoanalytical analysis of the motives behind Winter's choice of the word 'dream' confirms that, as Winter suspects, his real task lies in first understanding that which is real: the unreal, fragmented image of the world presented by television and advertising. Representing, as D'Angelo suggests, the spirit of early cinema, Alice's closer relation to the world of phenomena, her more direct access to the world, her uncomplicated understanding of things and her simplicity of vision are the tools that Winter lacks. Her role as guide and as visual therapist for Winter is never more clearly expressed than when Alice asks Winter to tell her something about himself while the two await a bus near Amsterdam airport. Winter cannot think of anything to tell, so Alice takes a Polaroid snap shot of him, handing it to Winter with the words 'So at least you know what you look like.' As Winter examines his likeness, Alice's face is reflected in the photo and becomes superimposed over his; while Winter so far seems to have little to offer Alice, except as a driver, this shot is a sign that Winter's and Alice's destinies are nevertheless closely intertwined, mostly because Winter is beginning to depend on and learn from Alice.

The block of 'dead' narrative time ends in Amsterdam with the realisation that it will be useless to wait for Alice's mother to arrive. Instead, Winter and Alice set off on a search for Alice's grandmother who, according to Alice, lives in Wuppertal. Winter rents a small car and the pair head off on their odyssey. Though the decision to start a search – coming after such a period of narrative stasis, in which we observe the characters eating, sleeping, even Winter having his hair cut – might at first be

FIGURE 8 *Alice in the Cities* (© 1974, Road Movies Filmproduktion GmbH)

interpreted as a sign that a more conventional narrative is about to begin, including elements such as purpose, tension, and possible narrative closure, this second half of the film simply renews the trajectory of the protagonists' movement from the first half of the film. We, the spectators, fall back into the role of searching and observing a new landscape through the window of a moving motor car. The grandmother is nothing more than a pretext for movement: Reinhold Rauh's detection of a new criminal element in the second half of *Alice in the Cities*, 'which gives rise to tension and makes all visible details meaningful',[10] is mistaken, not least because, unlike in *The American Friend* or *The End of Violence* which, from the beginning, exhibit some conventional criminal elements that introduce us to their narratives, there is never a hint of a potential threat to any of the figures in *Alice in the Cities*. This is altogether quite a different 'story'.

Winter's inability to see his life and his experiences as a cohesive whole that can be told as a story is clear from his reply to Alice when she asks about it in Amsterdam. Similarly, when Alice asks him to tell a story in the Wuppertal hotel, his response – he shouts at her 'I don't know any stories' – reinforces the point. However, Winter rethinks, takes a breath and then is able to summon up a story which alludes to Wenders' own method of storytelling. He begins, after some hesitation, with the classical beginning, 'Once upon a time...' and then relates a series of events that follow one another in steady succession. A little boy who goes for a walk with his mother gets lost in the woods. He meets a horseman, a truck driver and other characters and continues walking until he reaches the sea. Winter breaks the story off once Alice falls asleep. The beginning of this related story is a pretext for the succession of events that follow, just as the framework story about a man who meets a girl who's mother disappears is a pretext for the making of *Alice in the Cities*. The stations of the boy's adventure – each time he meets a new character in the forest – correspond to the episodic structure that characterises Winter's and Alice's adventures in the film until this point. The stories related by both Wenders and Winter are products of the succession of their episodes, and both stories have open beginnings – the little boy is already walking at the beginning of the story – and open endings.

But perhaps the most significant aspect of this sequence is that Winter had twice felt at a loss when Alice had made a demand on him that required storytelling. He could find nothing to tell her about himself in the form of a verbal account, nor did he feel he had a story to tell her at bedtime. Winter only feels able to tell a story, after some reflection, that is wholly invented: an approach to cinematic narrative that is formally consistent and thematically present throughout Wenders' work. Hanns in *Summer in the City* reflects that, in order to avoid reducing life to its highlights, he would need one year's time to describe the year he spent in prison: where should one begin the story, what should one leave out and what ought to be included? Robert in *Kings of the Road* replies to Bruno's question 'I want to know who you are' with the words 'I am my story'. Friedrich Munro in *The State of Things* dies for his conviction that 'stories only exist in stories (whereas life goes by without the need to turn it into stories)'. And Travis in *Paris, Texas* only feels able to tell his own story in the third person – as a 'real' story – with his back turned to the listener. These stories, when they are told, provide the teller and listener with a structured order to things – a form of cohesion which, Wenders admits, is comforting to the listener[11] – but that which is also artificial and imposed. As we have already discussed in earlier chapters, for Wenders, an artificially structured account of things in the form of a story brings 'lies, nothing but lies, and the biggest lie is that they show coherence where there is none'.[12] Which is why he claims to use stories such as the story outline of *Alice in the Cities* only as 'a hook for hanging pictures'.[13]

Finding images is, of course, what *Alice in the Cities* is about. Alice seems to have no memories of her past: she knows neither her grandmother's name nor her mother's maiden name, and she does not know where her grandmother lives. The few clues she does have are based on vision – she remembers that there were trees around the house – and on sound – the sound of soot crackling between the pages of her grandmothers' books. Most of all, her memories seem to be based on the photographs she carries with her of her grandmother's house and family members. These photos are placed on the dash of the rented motor car and begin to lead Alice and Winter in the right direction as concrete points of reference: the house as a kind of memory, a visual representation of the potential end of this search and of this narrative trajectory, the photograph of the mother possibly for inspiration, certainly as a memory stimulant for the spectator.

During their search for the house in Oberhausen, the camera sometimes follows Winter and Alice, and at other times adopts the perspectives of the two searchers. When the camera reproduces the point of view of the protagonists, Wenders uses tracking shots from inside the moving car, which are similar to shots in many of Wenders' student films such as *Same Player Shoots Again* and *Summer in the City*, in which characters are tracked as they walk along a road. Here, the camera observes the buildings in Oberhausen which, as Winter is informed by a local resident, would soon make way for a new hospital.

The sequence in Oberhausen encourages the spectator to share with Wenders the activity of pure contemplation through a camera simply directed out of a car window onto the rows of houses in a suburb of Oberhausen. The sequence becomes an autonomous episode because, as with the earlier scene atop the Empire State

Building in New York, the story and characters are, for the moment, forgotten, and the visuals take over as a form of descriptive narration. The spectator can sink, with Wenders, into the shared activity of still observation, meditation and contemplation – taking part in Wenders' search for pure images, and Winter's and Alice's search for home, even though the search is forgotten for the moment. This sequence is thus the opposite of what Grob describes as an 'ornamentalising' sequence because it neither attempts nor succeeds in detracting attention from the film images themselves or from the observing activity already in progress.

The search for the house in *Alice in the Cities* marks another important turning point in Winter's visual rehabilitation. Whereas before, he had always sought to catch an image of reality in his Polaroids, comparing his snapshots against the object he had photographed once they had developed, he immediately recognises the house from Alice's photograph, despite the fact that the vicinity and its inhabitants have changed since the photograph was made. He is astounded to find that the house exists. Even if the house and the area no longer look exactly as they do in the photograph, the important thing that Winter learns from this experience is that, unlike the snapshots of America, Alice has a connection to the object in the photograph: the image is the only link between a memory of a real past, a real story, and the reality of the existence of the house. Winter scratches his head: 'That's impossible!' He is astounded, not because of the likeness of the photograph to the house, but because the house, which had before been the still point of his movement with Alice, and had existed only as a tale and a photograph, concretely exists. The photograph, and the fact of the existence of the house, unifies the act of narration with actual reality, providing cohesion for an, until then, seemingly arbitrary representation of reality in a simple snapshot.

While Kolker and Beicken are correct in their assessment of images as being 'untrustworthy' substitutes for reality most of the time (this is true, for example, of Winter's Polaroids), they mistakenly assert that the 'picture of grandmother's house proved to be a disappointment insofar as its reproduction of the actual house could not satisfy the characters' desire to find the person formerly housed in this "real" building'.[14] In fact, Winter seems rather relieved to have found the house corresponding to the image: whether or not the grandmother still lives there is irrelevant, the house may no longer be the grandmother's house, but it is concretely there. Winter is relieved, above all, because he has learnt something about the nature of the relationship between images, stories and real experience, and because the story does not have to end here. The road continues on a short excursion across the Rhine in a ferry, and a train journey towards Germany's south. As the camera rises from a

FIGURE 9 *Alice in the Cities* (© 1974, Road Movies Filmproduktion GmbH)

close-up of Alice's and Winter's faces looking out of the window of the train, there is no suggestion of closure, only the suggestion of a possible continuation of the story, perhaps with Alice's mother in Munich. The aerial shot from the helicopter provides a glimpse of the landscape as far as the horizon, only to descend again in the next film, *Wrong Movement,* to the town of Glückstadt where we observe a young man named Wilhelm Meister, who also tries in vein to write, through the window of his room. Meister is also played by Rüdiger Vogler.

Alice in the Cities enters into a profound discourse on the production and consumption of images, and contrasts a number of conflicting approaches to film-making as well as to artistic production in general. Wenders uses his character and the thin outline of the film's story to be able to hold this discourse. While Winter's exasperation at the tendency in American television towards the commercialisation of images ('Every image wants something from you') is an evident and blunt attack on televisual aesthetics in general, including the role Wenders perceives it to have played in a similar aesthetic developing in conventional cinematic production, it is also a filmic reaffirmation, through Winter, of Wenders' own position regarding the influence of television on vision as an experience, as he describes in his poem 'The American Dream'.

FIGURE 10   *Alice in the Cities* (© 1974, Road Movies Filmproduktion GmbH)

Set against the backdrop of this inherently televisual notion of images is Winter's desire to be able to see clearly, to allow time for contemplation and reflection on his environment. This opposing force is represented in *Alice in the Cities* by the presence of John Ford in the discourse on image-making, is expressed in Winter's dream and in the comparatively uncomplicated, calm film images of Europe and Germany, and is embodied in Alice, whose clearness of vision allows her an uncomplicated and unopinionated understanding of her environment, and a respect for simple existence. While commenting that the photograph Winter takes from the window of the jet taking him and Alice to Amsterdam is 'so nice and empty', Alice directs Winter's attention at himself when she gives him the photograph of himself to contemplate who he is as the subject of an image, a unique phenomenon.

While Alice's perceptive qualities represent the opportunity for Winter to learn a new mode of vision, Wenders contrasts these qualities against the incoherence afflicting Winter's understanding of the visual world, and against modes of image production and consumption influenced by television aesthetics. This contrast defines and illustrates the nature of his alternative to the modern visual experience, and the role he perceives cinema could play in the realisation of this alternative. *Alice in the Cities* proclaims the death of the legendary and mythical American cinema of the 1940s and 1950s, killed off by the introduction of television and the new image-making aesthetic it brought with it. Rather than suggesting a revival of the old cinema, Wenders suggests a review of early cinematic practice (an image-based cinema descending from the pioneers, the Lumières, Skladanovskys, and others) coupled with the minimalistic and uncomplicated, yet strong narrative tradition represented by the qualities Wenders values in Ford's films.

On the visual level, *Alice in the Cities* thus finds the key to visual complexity to lie in visual simplicity, because a mode of film-making that respects the appearance of physical reality promotes observation and contemplation of the visible world as a worthwhile activity. On the level of film narrative, Wenders suggests an open, episodic, narrative form with a minimum of dramatic content to break the dominance that story has traditionally enjoyed over the image in film, thereby demanding attentive observation from the spectator, at the same time as making use of a narrative framework to attract the audience's attention and to provide a frame for the presentation of his images.

Paris, Texas

Critics such as Norbert Grob, Robert Kolker and Philip Beicken have categorised Wenders' work into three or more periods – an initial, formative period until *Kings of the Road*, a period featuring more conventional narrative until *Paris, Texas*, and an as yet only vaguely described third period 'with new heroes, new stories, new experiments'.[15] However, with regard to the undeviating discourse into the relationship between image and narrative in his films, Wenders' work is, from beginning to end, an ongoing exploration, an experiment in progress: one film is always a reaction to what came before, a new step, a new experiment, even though the form of presentation in the individual films may vary or seem to build thematic blocks.

Wenders' arrival at *Paris, Texas* thus represents neither more nor less the end of a phase or process, or the sum of all of Wenders' films to date, than any other of his films, but one more step forward in the investigation into cinematic form. The major formal and thematic influence on *Paris, Texas* was that which came immediately before: Wenders' experience of film-making in Hollywood with *Hammett*, and his reaction to this experience in *The State of Things*. In the latter film, Wenders had pushed himself into an extreme and decisive position, which he describes in the following terms:

In order to be able to visualise the free space in the middle [between the images], you need walls. After *The State of Things* I thought 'Now or never!'

Either I learn from this film to reject its thesis about the impossibility of stories, or I have no real future as a film-maker. That's why I tried to follow the script strictly in *Paris, Texas*.[16]

Paris, Texas addresses the conflict between image and narrative that had always been latent in Wenders' filmic discourse, but that came to a decisive peak in *The State of Things*, both in its structure and its theme: what kind of storytelling is possible in film without threatening the integrity of the image, and its primary function of rendering the world visible?

In *The State of Things*, Wenders found his theory that the space between the images in a film were enough to hold the film together to be flawed. Clearly in response to this dilemma, *Paris, Texas*, with a script written by the American actor/author Sam Shepard, exhibits one of the strongest narrative structures in any Wenders film, and recalls his experiments with stronger narrative structure in *The American Friend* and *Hammett*. Common to these three films is a clearly defined space in which the narrative unfolds. In the case of *Paris, Texas* this geographical space is triangular and incorporates western and southern territories of the US, from Houston and the Mexican border in the extreme south as far as Los Angeles in California on the West Coast. In contrast to Wenders' earlier films, in particular the road movies, the narrative develops within this enclosed space rather than following a line, as is the case in *Alice in the Cities*, *Kings of the Road* and *Wrong Movement*. *Paris, Texas* relies as much on dramatic tension as *The American Friend* and *Hammett*, and culminates in a dramatic peak at the end of the film. Though the film is open at both ends, the dramatic culmination – the apparently successful end of a search – lends the film a feeling of closure. The narrative moves within a self-contained geographical area and, at the end of the film, returns to where it began, giving it a united, circular form. It exhibits none of the *temps morts* of *The State of Things* or the earlier road movies, is generally quicker-paced and provides a good sense of the passage of time.

One important consequence of the boundaries of the narrative in *Paris, Texas* being fixed within borders is that the narrative space is divided into three separate units of space, much as the seemingly endless temporal trajectories of the road movies are divisible into units or episodes of time. *Paris, Texas* is a spatial film rather than a segment of time. This is partially responsible for the impression reflected in most critical writings on *Paris, Texas* that the film exhibits a more conventional narrative structure: emphasis is laid on each of the spaces – the desert of the beginning, Los Angeles in the middle and Houston at the end – where dramatic events relevant to the development of the narrative occur. In the road movies, such stations were less bases than they are in *Paris, Texas*, more places to be passed through and left. It is the division of the narrative space and the particular associations attached to each of the three spaces that make this structure particularly suitable for the theme of *Paris, Texas*, as the movement of the protagonists and the film between these spaces reflect Wenders' thematic concern: the search for a kind of narrative, a frame that allows the presentation of the film's images, without compromising their integrity.

The film begins in the desert of the American South-West. In the desert, vision is limited only by the sky itself: there are few landmarks and there is no language. The desert is, for these reasons, a place where a story, which requires language and points of reference, is nigh on impossible: in a film that follows a solitary character, not only is there no vehicle for the expression of the story, but its path would be aimless if there were. The unobstructed vision, and the lack of any recognisable landmarks in the desert sequence in the first half of *Paris, Texas* make the desert the realm of the image.

The second narrative space, centred on Los Angeles and the Henderson family home, is marked out by a completely different set of characteristics. It begins when Travis stumbles into a settlement called Terra Lingua. As the name of the town suggests, this is also the point at which language enters the film, and at which the spectators receive the first verbally communicated narrative information: that Travis is dumb, and has a relative in Los Angeles. Travis is led away from the vacuum of the desert into the new environment by his brother, Walt, who is most strongly associated with this new milieu. The desert clinic and the inside of Walt's car are the places where language resides. Walt moves in straight lines, is unwilling to depart from his course and would like to reach his destination as quickly as possible. From the moment of Travis' arrival at Walt's house in a Los Angeles suburb, almost all the narrative information until the end of the film is transmitted verbally. The more language begins to define the progress of the narrative, the stronger the presence of the narrative also becomes. At the same time, vision on the level of the film image becomes increasingly restricted the closer Walt and Travis come to Walt's home.

A third narrative space consists of an amalgamation of Travis' and Walt's spaces in form, beginning the moment Travis and his son, Hunter, leave Los Angeles for Houston. The road to Houston begins beneath a freeway bridge where several roads meet, symbolising the blending of chaotic with resolute movement through this space, and the fact that a decision is made here that will decide the shape of the future for the protagonists. To get to Houston, Travis re-enters the desert with Hunter but stays on the road. Though the destination is certain – a drive-in bank – neither figure knows for sure whether they will also find the object of their search, Jane, Travis'

FIGURE 11   *Paris, Texas*   (© 1984, Road Movies Filmproduktion GmbH)

wife and Hunter's mother. The combining of the desert and the inside of Travis'
car on the way to Houston leads to a camera use that reflects the contrasting spatial
dimensions at play: several wide shots on the landscape, and close-ups inside the car,
while medium shots are mostly used within hotel rooms and populated areas along the
route. Houston is presented as 'the opposite image to the desert in the beginning'[17]
and is where the strongest narrative elements develop. Travis and Hunter stake out a
bank in the hope of catching Jane as she comes to deposit money. This is immediately
followed by a car-chase sequence and the tension of not knowing whether the pair are
following the right car. Finally, we see Jane in the claustrophobic cubicle where she
works. Vision is most limited here, and the camera continuously seeks new angles on
the figures. Language flows freely both in Houston and at this most dramatic moment
from the point of view of the narrative in the film, which ends in a flood of words as
Travis relates the story of his life together with Jane.

The development of the theme of *Paris, Texas* is thus reflected in the film's
structure: on the search for a formula, a narrative structure that admits a story,
dialogue, and communication into the film while at the same time offering, even
promoting, the integrity of the filmic image. The film moves from a dead space, where
narration is impossible, but where vision on the level of the image is unlimited, to
inhabited or developed spaces, where the liberty of the image becomes increasingly

restricted spatially, and where the fact of communication – the presence of language – promotes the act of narration in the film.

On the level of the theme, however, *Paris, Texas* relies mainly on the characterisation of the protagonists, their association with the narrative spaces in the film, and on allusion for the discourse on images and story presented within this narrative structure. Travis Henderson is most strongly associated with the desert of the beginning, which characterises him with the same qualities that mark the desert. The figure of Travis is, through analogy and through his particular background, bound very much to the natural elements characterising the desert: as we are told at the end of the film, Travis walked away from his burning family home into the desert, where we and the film join him. His first action is to drink the water remaining in the plastic container that he carries, and then to seek new water from a dry tap in a settlement. One of the few possessions he carries with him is a photograph of a plot of land in the desert: the place where, he believes, he was conceived. His intention – to settle with his family on this plot – can be understood as an effort to preserve the continuity of his family heritage not just because of his assumption of having himself been conceived at this spot, but also because of his assumed Mexican-American family history. At the beginning, his sole companion is a falcon that watches him (a symbol of isolation and of the proximity of death, rather like a vulture). Because there are no landmarks in the desert, there is no specific direction to Travis' movement: the camera most often observes him as he walks through the image, moving through its depth. Travis wanders aimlessly and will not be able to leave the desert, the representation of his inner state, until he can leave his trauma behind him as well, which consists of dumbness, aimlessness, and vacuum. The numerous lines that bisect the image in the desert are a sign that both Travis and the film are searching for such a direction to follow. Travis walks only in straight lines until his brother, Walt, finally manages to convince him to get into the car. He ignores the roads and paths in the desert, crossing them without wavering from his course, and follows a railway track. In the first frames of the film he seems to be following the Mexican/US border (a doctor later asks Travis whether he knows which side of the border he is on). And once in Walt's car, still dumb, Travis traces the lines on a map with his finger until he finds Paris. This is the first word he says in the film (after twenty-three minutes).

Even more than the figure of Winter in *Alice in the Cities*, who was defined by extra-diegetical information, Travis appears with an extremely violent and traumatic experience behind him that has put him in a state resembling autism or some other emotional or intellectual rupture, the details of which are kept from the spectator until the very end of the film. But we nevertheless immediately sense the presence of some disturbance in Travis through his behaviour and appearance, his environment, and through the fact that this figure is in this environment. It is exclusively the acting and the images that convey to us this information, as Travis is completely alone in the desert, and he does not speak; he just walks through the empty landscape and through the image that accompanies him, away from the camera. Ry Cooder's blues guitar adds a sense of complete isolation to the overall picture we have of Travis at this point.

As soon as Travis moves from the desert into Walt's space – beginning in the desert clinic and including the inside of Walt's car, and the family home in Los Angeles – his character begins to react to the new environment, reflecting the changed conditions that characterise this space. This is where Travis slowly re-acquires language and the power of communication, which will be the most significant ability in the decisive Houston sequences from the point of view of the conclusion Wenders reaches regarding filmic narration. The closer Travis comes to Walt's house, the stronger his linguistic capabilities become. Walt and his wife, Anne, are associated with verbal communication from their first appearance – they speak on the telephone, and he and Anne are both observed clinging to the telephone in the film.

Similarly, the new direction that the story takes from the point at which Walt enters the story also benefits Travis, in that he gains the ability to direct his movement and intention towards reaching a certain goal: finding his estranged wife. His figure has clear psychological motivations for his actions, which are made plain to the viewer,

FIGURE 12 *Paris, Texas* (© 1984, Road Movies Filmproduktion GmbH)

and he seems to have a clear goal. This is mirrored in the film's story which, it seems, also begins to take shape here, in preparation for a conventionally determined goal of narrative culmination at the end of the film: the conclusion of the search that is begun here. The film's search for story, then, is expressed through its main character and his reaction to the environments in which he finds himself.

But Los Angeles is also the place where the part of the filmic discourse regarding images, which begins in the expanses of the desert at the beginning of the film, starts to take shape. The particular construction of the filmic space of *Paris, Texas*, and its division into three entities with different spatial dimensions, leads to a different camera use, and varying fields of vision within these spaces. Of these, the unrestricted vision in the opening desert sequences is presented as an ideal for vision, and is contrasted with the spaces where vision is limited due to spatial restriction and lack of light. These spaces – in particular the desert café and the booth where Travis finds Jane – convey an impression of imprisonment, restriction and confinement, and lead to a different kind of camera use and cutting techniques to deal with the changed spatial dimensions. Most significant of these is the greater use of a wide-angle lens in the restricted areas, which has the effect of significantly reducing depth of field in the image, when compared to telephoto or standard lenses.

It is inside these imprisoned areas that we find the subject Wenders chooses as his tool for his exploration of filmic images: commercialised images of women which, for Wenders, constitute the archetypal degraded image. Though Wenders has never shown an obvious awareness of feminist film theory, the images of women in *Paris, Texas*, with the exception of Walt's wife, Anne, reflect the feminist argument, put forward by Laura Mulvey, that women have traditionally been represented as little more than a surface in images, lacking a depth of their own, as a focus of male objectification in Hollywood and in Western society at large.[18] They equally conform to Wenders' assessment, which he gave in an interview with Taja Gut and published in *The Act of Seeing*, of commercial images as a form of 'violence or compulsion' because of the way the images are used, and because of the message this use attaches to them.[19] Wenders refers to this tradition when asked, in 1982, whether he could imagine making a film with a female lead:

It seemed easier for me to begin with male relationships, especially in the seventies. But that was just a preparation for me, and I hope, after a few films, to take a step forward and start telling stories about men and women. But I don't want to tell them in the accustomed way: that tradition is so false, so horribly and vilely false, especially where the women are concerned. It's very rare for women to be well portrayed in the cinema. Only very few directors have managed it. Antonioni is one of them.[25]

Both in the desert café and in Los Angeles, Travis is framed against semi-pornographic images of women. In the first example, Travis, exhausted from his aimless, but strangely purposeful trek through the desert, reaches the desert café. Instead of drinking beers from the refrigerator that he opens, he fills his mouth with ice from an ice-machine and promptly collapses. Behind him, hanging on the wall of this men's bar, is a reproduction of a reclining nude figure. Though the picture is far from being a pornographic work, the location, behind the drinks cooler in the male atmosphere of the bar, makes it stand out as if it were a page taken from some crude stripper or cheerleader calendar. The second, more directly revealing example is the figure of a reclining woman in a gymnastics costume, advertising mineral water, positioned on a giant billboard above a highway in Los Angeles. Both these images feature a degree of displacement or abuse of their subjects: the first – a potential work of art – is degraded to the role of sexual icon, stimulant, or gratification for male consumption because of its situation in the bar; the second image is an example of the commercial exploitation of women in advertising. Like the former image, this one, too, shows the woman as object and in fragments, lacking the depth of a third dimension (augmented by the

FIGURE 13 *Paris, Texas* (© 1984, Road Movies Filmproduktion GmbH)

use of a wide-angle lens that reduces depth of field), and is equally sexually iconic. For Wenders, these images, their two-dimensionality, are symbols of a prevailing misogyny in society, and expose the way in which the female image, degraded for commercial or some other gain, is readily available; the suggestion being that the image of Woman is first appropriated, then remoulded, imprisoned in the image to reach a certain goal, or to present another image with which the subject has no actual relation.

Here, again, the discourse regarding filmic images relies chiefly on the associations attached to them in the film: they appear where vision is most limited (in the second example, Travis turns away from the image to remark on how vision is clearer in the opposite direction). The second image is, moreover, associated with Walt, who works for the company that makes the billboards. While the first appears in the desert – the set for many of John Ford's films, so admired by Wenders – the second is in Los Angeles, the centre of the American film-making industry which, according to Wenders' commentary in *Reverse Angle: NYC March 1982*, is responsible for the production of an increasing number of degraded and degrading images.[21]

Mostly, though, it is through their association with Travis that these images contribute to the development of the theme in *Paris, Texas*. If, as Kolker and Beicken suggest, the images of women in the film reveal aspects of Travis' violence against Jane,[22] they also serve to show the process by which Travis learns something about this violence. Whereas he collapses directly before the first example in the darkness of the desert bar, he uses the second to support himself on the scaffold holding the giant billboard image. Standing directly before the image he is pleased, as he holds onto it, that he can see things more clearly from there.

Both the above instances of images depicting women prepare the spectator for the thematic climax – which coincides with the film's dramatic ending. Travis and his son, Hunter, decide to travel together to Houston to retrace their wife and mother, Jane. The only information they have is that she deposits cash at a bank on the fifth day of each month. Jane is first seen in a home movie at the Henderson family home – images of better times when she and Travis were still a couple. In a way, this is the opposite image to the desert of the beginning, along with Houston (chronologically, Travis' time in the desert begins immediately after the time the home movie was made). The whole Henderson family appears together on a wide, sandy beach. Water is plentiful, and Travis is surrounded by his family: symbolically, an ideal image as far as *Paris, Texas* is concerned. In Houston, conversely, Jane is always shot in enclosed spaces: her car, in the peepshow and the foyer at the peepshow, where there are no apertures to the outside world. At the very end, she appears with Hunter in a Houston hotel room, still imprisoned (the shape of the windows of the hotel room suggest incarceration), but there is a view of the outside world. The composition of these shots links Jane firmly with the two previous images of women in the desert café and in Los Angeles.

A much stronger such link, though, becomes apparent in the booth where she works. Not only is she separated from the outside world, she is also physically separated from Travis and the camera by a sheet of mirrored glass dividing the peepshow into two separate areas. Seen from Travis's and the camera's point of view, Jane appears as a prostitute set within the confining borders of a frame, giving the image an appearance similar to both earlier images of women. Jane is thus clearly identified as a victim of the same degradation that allows the use of images of women as objects for commercial gain.

Travis pays two visits to Jane in the peepshow. He leaves the first time, obviously distraught at the sight of what has become of her after the break-up of their marriage, but returns the next day. Travis confronts her and himself with the story of their violence in what could be described as a sort of confessional hearing. His speech offers evidence of the strong psychological motivation behind his actions, as well as providing the background information that informs the spectator of the reasons why Travis was wandering in the desert in the first place at the beginning of the film. He refers to Jane and himself in the third person and has only a crude intercom device through which to speak to Jane through the glass divide. He relates the story of his domestic life with Jane, describing their initial happiness, followed by Travis' gradual descent into jealousy and alcoholism which resulted from his conviction that Jane's refusal to show jealousy when Travis was away for longer periods was evidence that she was seeing other men. The news that Jane was pregnant, Travis says, temporarily gave him new impetus to work for the family again, but when Jane accused Travis of using the child to tie her down, Travis turned back to the bottle and became violent and increasingly suspicious, eventually tying Jane to the stove during the day and attaching a cowbell to her ankle at night to ensure that she could not escape. The story ends with Jane setting fire to the family home, which brings an abrupt end to their relationship. When he has completed the story of their life together, which enabled Jane to recognise for the first time that she was speaking to Travis, he arranges her reunion with their son in a Houston hotel room.

Travis created an image of his young and beautiful wife out of jealousy. Although she was always loyal to her husband, as far as we know, Travis' obsession with her and his jealousy meant that he became suspicious of her. Travis' dream of an ordinary family situation relates to a very American dream of settlement in the inhospitable wilderness of the desert, the American (and cinematic) expansionist tradition of the desert out-post, the fruitful conquering of the desolation of the Wild West with the common aims of family, home, work, and land: an honest American dream. But, according to Travis' tale, this dream soon became corrupted. Travis tells Walt and Hunter, in separate scenes, how his father had often joked that his wife, Travis' mother, was from 'Paris', waiting before destroying the exotic impression of such a statement by adding 'Texas':

> He wanted to see something else in her. It was like an illness. He looked at her, but he didn't see her. He saw someone else, and he told everyone she was from Paris. He started believing it himself. And she was ashamed for him.

The relevance of this background information to the film's story is that the same tendency to see someone in a person or thing other than actually exists, which Travis describes here as an illness, is that it seems to have survived into the next generation in Travis. In his imagination, Travis nurtured an ideal image of Jane as the perfect wife who looked after the household, bore him a child and loved her husband. Whenever Travis began to doubt this image, whenever the reality of the relationship no longer seemed to correspond to this image, he reacted violently to restore it. In other words, he exchanged Jane herself for an image that he had created of her in his mind, which he loved more than the real Jane. These circumstances lead Stefan Kolditz to describe *Paris, Texas* as:

> A picture-film … it's not only made of images that made the film world-famous – it's also about images: the images that men make of women … Travis is a man who can't handle the image he's made of his considerably younger wife. He thinks she is what she later – at least symbolically – becomes: a whore.[23]

Kolditz identifies as one of the themes of *Paris, Texas* the potential dangers involved when photographic images, or their subjects, are perverted in a way that separates the subject and its identity. Jane's condition in *Paris, Texas* is presented as a direct result of Travis' projection of an image of her in his mind that conformed more to his imaginary ideal than to the nature of the woman he was actually with, which Wenders uses thematically to make a statement about the abuse of images in general. Still, although Kolditz's conclusion that *Paris, Texas* is a film about images is correct, he does not go far enough beyond the banality of the love story of Travis and Jane to address the nature of the cinematic exploration in progress:

> If *Paris, Texas* really is the story of Travis, a man who wants to work off his guilt by reconstructing what he had destroyed, then the film tells the story about how

images just lead to new images. Travis had an image in his imagination that blinded him to reality, which he then destroyed. Now, four years later, he has a new – diametric – image in mind ... He unites Hunter with Jane, not because she's his biological mother, but because he wants to get rid of the image of his guilt, which he finally recognises at the end of the film.[24]

Paris, Texas is thus a film about images, about degraded images, and about the degraded images men can have of women. Images that are appropriated for advertising or taken out of their original contexts for any reason at all, face the danger of losing their meaning or having it altered, of dissolving in a pastiche of degraded images without an undoubted identity of their own, and lose the spirit of identity that is latent within them. Precisely this has happened to Jane in the background story to *Paris, Texas* (though it should be noted that the case of women is just the extreme of a general situation: Wenders is making a statement about any abuse of any images).

Wenders' character, Travis Henderson, representing as he does the average middle-class American male, is sent forth from a desert – an iconic, now dead and empty landscape that has come to symbolise the myth of Hollywood's entertainment industry and, for Wenders, the death of the myth of Hollywood – into (apparent) civilisation. In Los Angeles, the font of the American image-making tradition, Travis' brother, Walt, is a producer of advertising billboards that feature commercialised images of women. Wenders confronts his character with one of these, and Travis begins to understand something of the nature of his violence against Jane. Travis is then sent to Houston where, in a brothel representing the absolute in perversion of images, a kind of dark, underground purgatory where degraded images collect, he discovers Jane's fate (Wenders chose Kinski for the part of Jane because he felt she was a capable actress who had come to represent a sort of nymphet figure through her roles in semi-pornographic and erotic movies over the years).

In his summary, Kolditz ignores the symbolic nature of Travis' act, and the metalinguistic context of the film, thus concluding that Travis is merely trying to appease his guilt in returning Hunter to Jane. But the confession Travis directs at Jane in the penultimate sequence of *Paris, Texas* could equally represent a confession of the director, of Wenders, on behalf of the whole history of image-making, for having contributed to the degradation of photographic images in this way. Travis merely confesses, that is, he relates the story of his life together with Jane in simple terms. He returns Hunter to his mother and departs the scene. Kolditz concentrates on this dramatic conclusion at the end of the film, not considering that the film begins and ends with Travis who, having recognised his errors, drives away into the Texan night, still unable to fit into the civilised world, to leave his emotional desert.

The return of Hunter to Jane is only an apparent closure because *Paris, Texas* is really about a characteristic inherent in modern society that fosters and supports men like Travis, who are possessed by their need to acquire and maintain control not just over women, but who have been trained in the art of ownership and consumption – a tendency reflected in the portrayal of women in cinema, advertising and other visual media. The film is left open because this problem is not resolved by the confession of Travis/Wenders. This is just a beginning: a sign that the battle to restore and preserve the integrity of images is not lost, that Wenders has not resigned himself to defeat after the dilemmas surrounding his experience working in Hollywood on *Hammett* and resulting in *The State of Things*, and that the continuing degradation and inflation of images is, maybe, resistible.

From the point of view of story in film, Wenders claims to have made a new discovery with *Paris, Texas*:

I learned that stories really do exist – without us. They're like a river, and the film is a boat. Before I had just explored the tributaries, the brackish waters. Then I ventured out into the middle of the river. That was *Paris, Texas*. Once one has completely surrendered to this flow, the flow of storytelling, one gets to the sea. I've been looking for this experience over and over again since then.[25]

On one hand, Wenders is undoubtedly referring to the experience of relying on a strong narrative structure and script in *Paris, Texas*. But he also seems to have made a discovery regarding the questions he raised after *The State of Things* regarding the relationship between story and image: not just Travis' confession, but the whole film relies, in the end, on Travis regaining the power of language that enables him to tell a story, in simple terms, as a simple narration. This short story, which is not the story of the film, represents a form of narration that foregrounds a linear structure, and offers the coherence and order necessary for the telling of events in the form of a story. It is this order and coherence that Travis (and the film) lacked at the beginning of the film. In the context of the film's cinematographic exploration Wenders suggests, through Travis' monologue, that this kind of narration can co-exist with photographic images without threatening the integrity of the film image.

Tokyo Ga

That American culture, particularly American cinematic culture, was a formative influence on Wenders' work, as it was on the work of many of his European colleagues and contemporaries, is evident in Wenders' adaptation of American genres and styles in his films. But in 1972, when the foundations of his film aesthetic were already established, Wenders discovered the films of the Japanese director Yazujiro Ozu (1903–63). Less an influence than a confirmation of his own evolution as a film-maker, Wenders seems to have recognised in Ozu a director from an older generation, a foreign culture, with a universal film language that was closely related to his own.

Ozu is the Japanese director whose work most expresses traditional Japanese values, concentrating mainly on the daily lives and interpersonal relationships of the members of lower and middle-class families.[26] Particularly his later films are characterised by a striking economy of means such as an almost exclusive use of static camera, straight cuts and studio shooting, and drama sustained mostly by dialogue. Ozu is respected for his innovative use of on- and off-screen space and his decentred narratives, features that, in some ways, also characterise Wenders' work.

Ozu's consistent violation of the classical 180° rule, for example, means that objects and backgrounds within the frame change frequently, lending these a more prominent presence in the image and forcing the viewer to pay more attention to setting in order to avoid confusion.[27] In combination with this use of space, Ozu tends to extend the spatial limits of the film frame in order to imply the existence of off-screen space by concentrating the centre of the image on objects that have no direct narrative importance. Though such objects as a vase or an empty room might themselves be meaningless in terms of narrative development, they draw attention to the surrounding space which, through off-screen sound for example, are emphasised as meaningful, containing meaningful objects or people.[28] In Wenders this technique is used to combat the illusionistic effect of centred framing, which effectively denies the existence of space beyond the limits of the image frame. The flying bird sequence in *Alice in the Cities* is one example of how Wenders uses objects unimportant to narrative development in order to draw attention away from the progression of the story and to the wider, visual environment.

De-emphasis of narrative peaks is another way in which Ozu's narrative style resembles that of Wenders. Discussing Ozu's film *Tokyo Story* (*Tokyo Monogatari*, 1953), Bordwell and Thompson refer to Ozu's incorporation of 'ellipses' at vital moments in the story, which reduces the impact of important narrative events. For instance, we hear about, but are not shown, the death of the grandmother, one of the main characters of *Tokyo Story*: 'The result is a shift in balance. Key narrative events are de-emphasised by means of ellipses, whereas narrative events that we do see in the plot are simple and understated.'[29] Although their techniques may differ, the de-emphasis of narrative impact and the emphasis on diegetical and non-diegetical visual phenomena are features common to both Wenders and Ozu, suggesting that they share an aesthetic basis regarding their respective evaluations of the relationship between image and narrative in film.

Wenders has usually referred only to Ozu's narrative style when describing what he found to mark Ozu's films apart from others. He claims to have learnt from Ozu 'that it makes no sense to try to force a story on a film. I've learned from Ozu that you can have a narrative film without a "storyline"'.[30] Yet while Wenders praises Ozu's films for their narrative qualities it is, above all, images of Ozu's Tokyo that he hopes to find in *Tokyo Ga*: 'I wondered whether I could still detect any traces of the time, whether there was anything left of that work, images, or even people.'[31]

The first impressions present a city and a population in constant movement: sounds from video arcades, pachinko halls, and televisions, augmented by the ever-present, discordant soundtrack, the constant rush of traffic, of trains and of the people in the Metro system that create a flood of images, and an inescapable cacophony of audio impressions that blend into a monstrous chaos. One contemplative shot early in the film exemplifies the sense of chaotic movement: the camera is held steady for exactly one minute and represents a completely independent, non-aligned point of view over a city-scape in which five passenger trains move across the screen from the left and the right. These cut a horizontal axis across the image which is bisected by cars travelling underneath the railway track on a vertical axis. Towards the top of the image another road can be seen leading diagonally across the screen. The whole picture is an impressionistic picture of life in the city of Tokyo and stands out of the bulk of the film because of the length of the shot, and because of the patterns of movement along the solid lines of the roads and the railway tracks.

In a second sequence of this kind, the shot is held for two minutes and thirty seconds and again features trains, but this time the shot is composed from the inside of a train, and frames another that is travelling on a parallel axis. Because of the darkness the train itself is not clearly visible, only the lights inside, and the reflections of the lights in the train carrying the camera are visible, creating patterns with moving and stationary lights. When the train can no longer be seen, Wenders raises the camera to observe the patterns of lights created by the movement of the train in which he is sitting past an illuminated tower-block.

FIGURE 14 *Tokyo Ga* (© 1985, Road Movies Filmproduktion GmbH)

Only three peaceful sequences in these first twenty minutes of the film break up the chaos: the familiar shot out of the window of the jet taking Wenders to Tokyo (contrasted by Wenders with the movie being shown aboard the jet), a group of people picnicking in a cemetery (the place of the dead) and a rebellious little boy in the Tokyo Metro, who refuses to take another step (contrasted with the people rushing past him).

In Wenders' voice-over commentary, he analyses the rift he perceives between the images of Ozu's Tokyo and his own first impressions of this audio-visually over-loaded environment, reflecting that the identity-forming function of images may have become lost in the inflation of visual impressions. In the film, this connection between images and identity is blatantly stated. However, having witnessed the chaos of Tokyo, Wenders expresses his fears that 'images that can unite the world, and are at one with the world, perhaps they are gone forever'.[32]

The insertion of this reflection on images and identity in his commentary between two sequences featuring television sets ('still more din for the eyes and ears') situates television as a primary factor in the loss, or even corruption, of the identity of an entire nation, evidenced in the chaos that characterises life in Tokyo (in this respect, it is significant that Ozu was active as a director throughout the period in which television was commercially introduced). In the first of these sequences, the television set is in a taxi moving along a road, which links it with the chaos of the city. The second is in a hotel room; after a John Wayne film the Japanese flag appears on the screen and the national anthem is played, prompting Wenders to reflect:

> Where I am now is the centre of the world. Every shitty television set, no matter where, is the centre of the world. The centre has become a ludicrous idea, and the world as well. An image of the world: a ludicrous idea the more television sets there are on the globe. And here I am, in the country that builds them all for the whole world, so that the whole world can watch the American images.

Television, the primary disseminator of American images and American lifestyle, Wenders implies in this film, is responsible for the inflation of meaningless images and the resulting confusion of identity afflicting the Japanese in Tokyo. A vehicle for the export of a dominant, commercially-oriented culture, television claims to bring all the world into the living room. But if the choice of what kind of images of the world are promoted is the result of a commercial calculation, then identity is formed and fixed on the basis of this commercial calculation, leading to a dysfunction: a confusion of identity.

Wenders sees this confusion of identity expressed in many trends in Japanese city life that seem to imitate other cultures, mainly European and American. He visits a golfing range on the roof of a Tokyo building, where hundreds of men and women who, he says, will probably never get to see a real golf course, practice their swing: 'But I was still astonished to see it demonstrated, as a balletic exercise, for the beauty and perfection of the movement. The point of the game, pushing the ball into a hole, seemed to have fallen into disrepute.'[33] After meeting Werner Herzog atop the Tokyo broadcasting tower (which eerily resembles Paris' Eiffel Tower), Wenders breaks off a visit to the newly-opened Disneyland Park on the outskirts of the city saying 'the thought of seeing an exact copy of the park in California made me reconsider, and I did a U-turn'. Later still, in a Tokyo park, youths outfitted in appropriate 1950s costumes gather to dance American rock 'n' roll dances. Finally, as if to show that the inclination towards cultural imitation had also begun to effect authentically Japanese cultural life, Wenders shoots a lengthy sequence, inter-cut with images from the inner-city golfing range, of a factory that manufactures wax imitations of Japanese dishes for display in restaurant windows.

From the point of view of his search for images of Ozu's Tokyo, Wenders realises that he will only succeed in finding his own images here: the difference between Ozu's and Wenders' perspectives on the city is illustrated in the sequence when Wenders imitates Ozu's composition in a Tokyo street that regularly appeared in Ozu's films: 'The result was a completely different scene, one that was no longer mine.'[34] This experiment – the imitation of a visual code alien to Wenders the film-maker – confirms Wenders' fears that Tokyo had embraced a new identity since Ozu's death, one that requires a new visual code to catch its essence. In this sense, Wenders' search in Tokyo for images of the past is futile since there are, presumably, only new images that exude a new national identity. Or, more probably, the experiment illustrates the futility of Wenders' attempt to find Ozu's Tokyo in concrete images of the present-day city.

Indeed, the only images in *Tokyo Ga* that concretely link Ozu's films with those of Wenders, that make a link between the past and the present, seem to be the frequent appearance of trains. In Ozu, the arrival and departure of trains habitually symbolises Japan's progress from a (war-torn) mainly agricultural society towards a modern industrial nation (that now produces televisions for the whole world). Film-historically, Klaus Kreimeier notes, trains have tended to symbolise modern alienation in the period of industrialisation.[35] In this sense, Ozu's films, which document Japanese life over a period of over thirty-five years, could be considered to present an image of Tokyo on the way to becoming the alienated and alienating city that Wenders experiences in the fragmentary chaos of modern Tokyo.

Wenders suspects early on in the film that he may be looking for something other than images of a past city or way of life in *Tokyo Ga*:

> The more the reality of Tokyo appeared as a wanton, loveless, menacing, even inhuman proliferation of images, the greater and more potent was the lovingly ordered mythical city of Tokyo in the films of Yazujiro Ozu, in my memory. Perhaps it was no longer possible: a perspective that was able to order an ever more terrible world, a perspective that could still produce transparency. Perhaps that was more than an Ozu of today could manage. Perhaps the hectic inflation of images has already destroyed too much.[36]

From Wenders' comments, it is maybe less a question of finding images that remind him of Ozu's Tokyo than of finding an attitude towards the given reality: Wenders' initial impressions of an overwhelming chaos are reflected in the disordered sequences of *Tokyo Ga* because, in this diary film, he is above all seeking to make his own confusion plain to the spectator, to show the chaos of the city. His attitude (*Einstellung*) towards the reality of Tokyo is therefore intended to reveal these impressions, with the result that his own film is a relatively unstructured sequence of chaotic impressions,

FIGURE 15 *Tokyo Ga* (© 1985, Road Movies Filmproduktion GmbH)

of fast-moving images and jumbled sounds. This is the form he employs in order to express these impressions, and his fear that a view capable of providing order has disappeared, also refers to his own view of the city, his own inability to hold up the flow of continually changing impressions.

The main difference between *Tokyo Ga* and the films of Ozu in this respect is that, in his films, Ozu's intent is to become closely involved in, above all, a set of characters that remain more or less constant throughout his film-making career, whereas Wenders does not attempt, for the purpose of this film, to become involved with individual figures. In other words, Ozu's objective had been to tell stories about the people of Tokyo, and Wenders' objective is to show life in the city from the point of view of a first-time visitor, an outsider. In this sense, Wenders is acting out Philip Winter's role as the alienated European in the US in *Alice in the Cities*, transposed to a different geographical location, particularly in view of his and Winter's comments on television in the respective films. Where Winter looks to Alice for a way of ordering his visual impressions in the former film, here Wenders looks to Ozu for ways of making sense of the city chaos.

The difference in Wenders' and Ozu's approaches, which determine the nature of their respective 'views' on Tokyo, are made clear in the two instances in *Tokyo*

FIGURE 16 *Tokyo Ga* (© 1985, Road Movies Filmproduktion GmbH)

Ga when Wenders does in fact attempt to achieve a degree of intimacy with figures from Ozu's film world: in the interview with Ozu's lead male actor, Chishu Ryu, Ryu describes Ozu as the 'master' whose disciplined working methods left his imprint on everything around him:

> In the studio, for instance, he not only concerned himself with the sets and decorations in general, but with every detail and every little thing. He positioned every cushion and put every little object in its place. Nothing was left to chance. He even straightened out the actors' costumes just before a take. And there's nothing wrong with that ... when someone is so sure of what he wants.[37]

Ozu's cameraman, Yuharu Atsuta, also gives a picture of Ozu as a director so obsessed with order, control and meticulous planning that he timed every shot exactly to the second with a specially designed stopwatch. Atsuta sets up a camera to show the low shooting position usually adopted in interior shots, which gave the impression that the camera was amongst the figures, one of the guests, allowing a spirit of intimacy to develop between the audience and the protagonists (and between the director and the actors).

These remarks are revealing in the context of Wenders' search in *Tokyo Ga*, and of his cinematic exploration into the incompatibility of images and story in film. If one accepts Wenders' claim in an interview with Jan Dawson that Ozu was the only film-maker he had learnt from 'because his way of telling stories was so completely representational',[38] and his evaluation in *Tokyo Ga* that Ozu possessed 'a view capable of providing order',[39] then it would be a reasonable deduction that it was above all an aspect of Ozu's narrative style that Wenders was hoping to find in Tokyo. The simplicity of Ozu's aesthetic of representational narration, which emphasises the visuality of events and phenomena in his films through careful and thorough attention to composition and strict control over time, to which Ryu and Atsuto's comments testify, and through the incorporation of off-screen space into the diegesis, confirms Wenders' own mistrust of stories and respect for the appearance of physical reality in film. At the same time, Wenders realises in *Tokyo Ga* that a concept of 'order', the necessity of a story to act as a frame for the presentation of images in film, is the key to promoting a sense of stability and identity, and to his being able to make sense of the chaos of Tokyo. This observation also confirms Wenders' position regarding the structuring function of stories expressed in the film *Reverse Angle: NYC March 1982*: 'Without the brace of a story, images are starting to look interchangeable and purposeless to me.'[40]

The importance of Ozu and of *Tokyo Ga* in Wenders' oeuvre is not restricted only to confirmation of a film aesthetic, but is of significance for the forward development of Wenders' aesthetic. The complexity of the multi-layered soundtrack of *Tokyo Ga*, in which ambient noise, commentary and score are audible simultaneously to express the chaos and disconnectedness of life in Tokyo is employed and functions similarly at the beginning of Wenders' next film, *Wings of Desire* (dedicated, in part, to Ozu). And, like in *Tokyo Ga*, Wenders resumes the search for an appropriate form to enable cinema, represented by the angel Damiel, to integrate the chaos of audio and visual impressions into the structure of a story that, as in the films of Yazujiro Ozu, nevertheless allows the image (and sound) to act as the chief information carrier and guardian of identity.

Wings of Desire

Against the background of Wenders' work, *Wings of Desire* shares many of the characteristics of the two feature films previously discussed:, *Alice in the Cities* and *Paris, Texas*. It has been described as a road movie of sorts, yet the film never departs from the location of the city of Berlin. It is filmed in black and white as well as colour.

It thematises both image and the search for a story and, representing a homecoming for a director who had spent the previous ten years working in America, exhibits a similarly restless tension between European and American cultural identity as any of the previous films.

At the same time, Wenders explores new technical and formal possibilities in *Wings of Desire*, for instance the use of a complex multi-track soundtrack to combine sound on several different levels simultaneously: 'I've never done something where the sound alone is already an entire film ... where there's so much to hear simultaneously, because so much is being told',[41] he admits. On the level of the image, this is the first film in which both black and white and colour are used, each stock type functioning as narrative devices. In some sequences, the image changes from black and white to colour within a shot, which, due to the restrictions this technique implies in the use of filters, has the effect of a visibly inferior image quality in these shots (quite a sacrifice for a director who places so much emphasis on the image in his films). The simulation of the incorporeal angels' point of view in *Wings of Desire* also meant a degree of technical innovation: the camera had to learn to fly and to move through solid objects.

In the first project description of *Wings of Desire*, written in 1986 and first published in English in the volume *The Logic of Images*, Wenders offers an insight into his hopes for the new film to catch something of Berlin's history and atmosphere, the sheer visibility of the city's history, as well as his own impressions of the city after his ten-year absence:

> A film that might convey something of the history of the city since 1945. A film that might succeed in capturing what I miss in so many films that are set here, something that seems to be so palpably there when you arrive in Berlin: a feeling in the air and under your feet and in people's faces, that makes life in this city so different from life in other cities.[42]

Later in the same text, the phenomenon of the city's historic division into east and west becomes an ever more dominant theme of the project description.

> Berlin is divided like our world
>
> ...
>
> The name of the film will be:
>
> THE SKY OVER BERLIN
>
> Because the sky is maybe the only thing,
>
> That unites these two cities

Apart from their past
of course. Will there be a common future?
'Heaven only knows'.[43]

Both this description of an original idea and many aspects of the film itself would seem to encourage an interpretation of the film as an idealistic call for an end to the division of the city – hence of the country and of the Cold War world. It contains the first images of destruction and death during the Second World War in Wenders' films, and the Berlin Wall, which two of the main protagonists, the angels Damiel and Cassiel (and Wenders' camera) pass through or over with ease, is an ever-present reminder of the city's division. Added to this are the characterisations of Damiel and the third main protagonist, Marion, as two opposites seeking to unite: Damiel, the angel, could be read as pure (incorporeal) spirit (East), and Marion, a circus trapeze artist, as pure material seeking a spiritual dimension (West). Both these figures seem incomplete, each one desiring experience of the attributes that characterise the other.

In their article, 'Handke's and Wenders' *Wings of Desire*: Transcending Postmodernism', David Caldwell and Paul Rea expand the idea of a united city/nation as a possible theme of *Wings of Desire* (which, admittedly, seems more acceptable as an interpretation since the historical reality of German reunification in October 1990) to comment on the film in the context of divisions and opposites in general.[44] The article contends that Wenders moves beyond the stability of the paired binaries of modernism (east/west, man/woman, black and white/colour, angelic/human, past/present, and so on) which, they say, he exploits in *Wings of Desire*, to seek a new order and stability in reciprocals. Caldwell and Rea place particular emphasis on image and word as opposite modes of experiencing, transcribing, and narrating knowledge and history.[45] Berlin, its particular history, and its way of going about with it, is the field in which this experiment takes place. The main protagonists, Damiel, Cassiel, Marion, and the two 'angelic' human figures Homer (Curt Bois) and Peter Falk, represent different ways of experiencing the world and they all expose a degree of perceptional dissatisfaction.

The word 'angel' derives from the ancient Greek *anghelos*, meaning messenger (Cassiel/Raphaela also refer to themselves in their monologue as 'the messengers' in the sequel film, *Far Away, So Close*).[46] The angel is the bearer of meaning: the signifier. The term consequently also suggests the existence of a space in, across or through which the message is conveyed: the space between the speaker and those to whom he speaks. The only function of Wenders' angels is to formulate, transport and deliver a message that consists of the events they witness based on vision and hearing. The choice of angels for the central figures in *Wings of Desire* was, according to Wenders, inspired by several different events: Rilke's *Duino Elegies*, Paul Klee's works, Walter Benjamin's essay 'The Angel of History',[47] a pop song by The Cure, and the Friedensengel (Angel of Peace) atop the Victory Column in Berlin: a mixture of different sources of inspiration from German art and literary history, and British pop music.[48] There is no mention in any of Wenders' texts of a religious background to the use of angels in the film, or that these angels, Damiel and Cassiel, represent the spirits of individuals who have died. Though their appearance and artificial, at times poetic, language suggests the presence of a religious background to their characterisation, these are no spiritual beings in the biblical sense. This is in stark contrast to their characterisation in *Far Away, So Close*, which ends with a monologue by Cassiel/Raphaela in which the spectator is offered closeness to a being referred to as 'Him'.[49] In *Wings of Desire*, all the central characters are angels in a way.

From the opening frames until the middle of the film the camera usually adopts the perspective of the angels. After the initial shot of a text which is being written, the film cuts to a shot on Damiel's eye in close-up, then dissolves into images of the city from an elevated point of view, thus identifying the camera with Damiel's point of view. Remaining mainly with Damiel's point of view in the first hour of the film, we follow his floating journey around Berlin, descending first to street level from the spire of Berlin's Gedächtniskirche (Emperor William Remembrance Church), then ascending into the sky and an aeroplane, then past a telecommunications tower into residential buildings where Damiel and the camera, which follows his point of view, move freely from one apartment to the next, through walls and across open spaces. Due to the seemingly random character of what we and Damiel see, we are at first unable to make much sense out of the pattern of events, except that we know we are being shown these events by Damiel, an angel. Beyond this realisation, the spectator has little to do other than watch the images and listen to the soundtrack. We are also able to catch seemingly random patterns of thought and speech from the characters that Damiel follows or observes, including even the multi-lingual broadcasts from the Berliner Funkturm (broadcasting tower) as we fly past. Were it not for the presence of the spiritual angels, this first part of the film would seem like its director had simply turned on a camera with a microphone and walked randomly through the city, its buildings, underground, and its streets – a sequence that seems to hark back to Wenders' earliest days at film-school in Munich, when the simple act of recording something for its own sake, the magical reproductive abilities of the camera, was the fascination for him.

The first time Damiel meets his colleague Cassiel in a car showroom, each presents his notebook and reads their observations in the form of a list, occasionally pausing to comment on the events they report. Cassiel's notes include events ranging from sunrise and sunset times, an air disaster in the 1960s, a man walking along the street who turned to look into the emptiness behind him, and a prisoner who said 'Now' while committing suicide. In this way, the messenger acts as a kind of memory that captures past events that seem noteworthy to the angels, preserving phenomena in a form that can be accessed in the future.

This sequence constitutes the first opportunity in the film for the spectator to make sense of the stream of constantly changing, seemingly random sounds and images, though the recognition that these are merely events witnessed by the angels is a relatively unspectacular revelation that does not yet contribute to the development of a recognisable narrative.

The second time Damiel and Cassiel meet to deliberate on past events they chronicle the local evolution, including the rise and fall of mankind in a kind of allegory. At this point it becomes clear that the angels have existed and been active in this location since the beginning of time. More importantly for the characterisation of the angels, though, they are also able to experience particular moments in time as if they were the present, to relive the past, jumping from one era to the next, an ability that is first apparent to the spectator when Cassiel observes the inserted documentary footage of destruction in the Second World War as if it were the present while riding through the city in a vintage car.

As the messenger, the angel does not just witness these events; he also records them in his memory, or writes them down in the form of notes in a notebook. The identification of the angel's eye with the camera's point of view, and their activity of observing, recording and re-telling, make the angels in *Wings of Desire* personifications of a cinematic ideal: a cinema based on the undiscriminating observation of all kinds of phenomena, in the world of physical appearance, the capturing of the secret of existence in photographic images, and the preservation of these images for the future. Norbert Grob has compared the work of Wenders' angels to the similar way Handke picks up on the smallest of details in his novel, *A Moment of True Feeling*:

In the sand at his feet [Keuschnig] saw three things: a chestnut leaf; a piece of a pocket mirror; a child's barrette. They had been lying there the whole time, but then suddenly they came together and became miraculous objects. 'Who said the world has already been discovered?' It had been discovered only in respect to the mystifications some people used to defend their certainties

FIGURE 17 *Wings of Desire* (© 1987, Road Movies Filmproduktion GmbH)

from others. [...] All the sublime mysteries ... were man-made, designed to intimidate people. But these wishing objects on the ground in front of him did not intimidate him. They put him in so confident a mood that he couldn't sit still. He scraped his feet on the ground and laughed ... I haven't discovered a personal mystery in them, addressed to myself; what I've discovered is the IDEA of a mystery valid for all! ... Since there was no need to wish anything more from the three objects, he scraped sand over them. [...] I've finally had an IDEA. He felt all-powerful again, but no more powerful than anyone else.[50]

In the translation of the angel's point of view through the camera, Wenders insisted upon an 'attitude to an attitude, a caring attitude',[51] which points towards an attempt at maintaining the respect for ordinary, as well as spectacular, phenomena in the image, an attempt at accessing the 'mystery valid for all' described in Handke's text. In particular, the timelessness of the angels' existence cements the parallel with the cinematic image due to cinema's status as a recording art. This interpretation of the angels' function in the film is supported by Wenders' description of cinema in *The Act of Seeing* as an 'archival activity':

Without question. Sometimes you only notice afterwards, but sometimes it's done quite consciously ... The fact that something is due to go is always a good reason to include it in a scene. *Wings of Desire* is full of examples. Almost none of our locations exist any more. Starting with the bridge where the motorcyclist dies. That's gone.[52] The place where we had the circus is now a park. No need to mention Potsdamer Platz. Or the Wall either. The whole film suddenly turned into an archive for things that aren't around any more. Films that don't call themselves documentaries, feature films, do that to an amazing degree.[53]

Film has the same capability as the angels to hold a record of past events and of objects that change or disappear over time, and to make their appearance available for viewing in the future. The fact that film images are restricted to recording an illusion of reality is also mirrored in the angels. Like the camera in a film, the angels are invisible observers, and like a photographic image, they do not come into actual contact with the world, but, with their black and white vision, can only capture images of the physical appearance of things, seeing things and people like shadows on a cinema screen, or they physically handle ghostly outlines of objects, not the objects themselves (for example when Damiel attempts, in separate sequences, to pick up a stone and a pen, the actual objects remain in position, Damiel can only examine their image). The film's dedication ('Dedicated to all the former angels, but especially to Yazujiro [Ozu], François [Truffaut] and Andrei [Tarkovsky]') crystallises the identification of the angels with a cinematic tradition of the *Autorenfilm* within which Wenders locates himself.

The angels exist in a domain parallel to that of the humans. They are able to observe humans, and are even capable of communicating with them on a spiritual level. It seems that they are visible to some of the child characters in the film. On three occasions, Damiel manages to access the consciences also of adult humans: he places his hand on the abdomen of a woman who is about to give birth, lessening her pain; he consoles a man in an underground train, who sees a bleak future, helping him to feel more positive about his domestic situation; and he begins to recite a songlike poem, which a man continues to recite before his death after a motorcycle accident. But, by and large, the angels do not seem able to influence events in the human world, which Cassiel painfully learns when he is unable to prevent a suicide attempt. The narrative core of *Wings of Desire* is situated between these two worlds, and the film's thematic thrust is built from the tension that exists between the ethereal world of the angels, and the generally bleak life led by the humans in their world.

And that is the problem for Wenders' cinema: humans – the intended recipients of the angels' message – are blind to the everyday phenomena recorded by the angels, yet they seek constantly refreshed sensations elsewhere. In an interview with Wenders,

Gerd Gemünden remarks on the moral aspects of Wenders' films, making the suggestion that morality had to do with

> a certain respect for objects and locations in which the characters move. It seems you want to do justice to the things you show on the screen, and the films take their time in order to achieve this. In your last two films the moral aspect has been transposed from the level of form to the level of content. Many critics saw this as a lack of subtlety. One spoke of Wim Wenders as a moralist who is primarily concerned with delivering a message.[54]

Wenders agrees with Gemünden, adding that 'the images can no longer carry the message'.[55] But, rather than ascribing a deficiency to film images themselves, Wenders gives vent to his frustration, suggesting that their inability to carry a message is related to the dominant modern cinema aesthetic of entertainment:

> The hesitancy to say something rests on the inability to form an opinion. Everybody wants to stay out of things. But with the present situation, one cannot stay out of things. Today, films are evaluated exclusively by their entertainment value, and it bothered many people that *Far Away, So Close* had a message, especially if they saw it as a Christian message.[56]

Both image and soundtrack in *Wings of Desire* illustrate the particular form of blindness Wenders describes above. The inner monologues of the Berliners in the first hour of the film, which we hear as Damiel's hearing, go to the heart of the matter: men and women are plagued by their everyday problems; children are, like the angels, in their own dreamy world (a violent domestic dispute is seen to alienate a child from its family); and we are witness to the last thoughts of a man who kills himself. These captured thoughts are blended with other sounds from radios, the ever-present television sets and the multi-lingual broadcasts from the Funkturm (broadcasting tower) – a modern-day tower of Babel. Two children argue about the television show *Wetten Daß* (*You Bet!*), while others spend their time playing video games.

Only for the angels do the everyday and ordinary phenomena seem to hold some fascination, or to promise sensation. The Berliners themselves are full of doubt. And it is the angels – and therefore the cinema – that is cited here as a force capable of removing doubts, that holds the promise of answers, if only the audience were less blind: Wenders' cinema – the messenger – has lost its audience and recipient to the pace of modern-day life, and has become near to irrelevant. The audience has lost a mode of vision, which the angels can provide. Cassiel bemoans his spiritual existence: 'To be alone! Let things happen! Be serious! ... To do no more than look, assemble, testify, preserve! To remain spirit! Keep your distance! Keep your word!'[57] The activities of the angels seem senseless when described in this way: though they continue to collect their records of occurrences from day to day, they can make no use of their note-taking, other than for self-reflection. Cassiel's sentiments bare a striking resemblance to Wenders' own verdict on his work until 1982. Speaking after the making of *Paris, Texas* in 1984, Wenders alludes to Cassiel's words when he claims to have made 'quite a number of films that were more concerned with reflecting themselves than reflecting anything that exists apart from movies. And I think that's a really serious dead-end for something that I love very much, which is movies.'[58]

It is this lack of effectiveness and loss of relevance that seems to weigh heavily on Damiel's conscience. This perceived impotence is expressed diegetically in one of the sequences shot in Berlin's State Library when we can listen in to one of the readers, the 'Second Reader', as he reads from a book about Walter Benjamin's purchase in 1921 of Paul Klee's water-colour, *Angelus Novus*. Benjamin interprets the water-colour in his text *Theses on the Philosophy of History* as an allegory of a glance back at history. Of the painting, Benjamin says:

> A Klee painting named *Angelus Novus* shows an angel looking as though he is about to move away from something he is fixedly contemplating. His eyes are staring, his mouth is open, his wings are spread. This is how one pictures the angel of history. His face is turned toward the past. Where we perceive a chain of events, he sees one single catastrophe which keeps piling wreckage upon wreckage and hurls it in front of his feet. The angel would like to stay, awaken the dead, and make whole what has been smashed. But a storm is blowing from Paradise; it has got caught in his wings with such violence that the angel can no longer close them. This storm irresistibly propels him into the future to which his back is turned, while the pile of debris before him grows skyward. This storm is what we call progress.[59]

The desire to find ways of gaining new relevance will eventually lead Damiel to surrender his spiritual existence in return for experience of the human world. His motives and sources of temptation are many. During the first meeting with Cassiel, he expresses the desire to give his existence some relevance:

It's great to exist as the spirit, to testify, day by day and forever on the spiritual in peoples' minds. But I do get tired of my spiritual existence, of forever hovering above. I wish I could grow a weight which … could bind me to Earth. I wish I could say, at each step, each gust of wind, 'Now'. Say 'Now' and 'Now' and no longer 'Forever' and 'For eternity' … Every time we participated it was pretence … No, I don't have to beget a child or plant a tree. But it would be rather nice … for once to find excitement not in the mind but in a meal, in the line of a neck, in an ear … to feel your bones moving as you walk … To feel what it's like to take off your shoes under a table, and to wriggle your toes, like this.[60]

Damiel's subjective postulation is that closer contact to the physical world – more than just observing objects and events – is a solution to the crisis of irrelevance and ineffectuality. His world is, if not purely spiritual, the world of non-material perception (light, shadow and thought) and he makes the decision to join the human world partly in order to gain experience of physical matter. This desire is illustrated in a sequence in Marion's caravan. Damiel follows Marion from the circus tent to her trailer, listening all the time to her thoughts. In the caravan, Damiel turns his back on Marion to pick up and fondle a stone that is lying on a table. He can, however, only pick up its likeness, the stone itself remains on the table. He turns it over, tosses it in his hands as if trying to feel its weight and texture, whilst Marion, sitting on her bed, begins to undress behind him. He turns around and, still holding the image of the stone in his hand, traces the line of Marion's neck and shoulder with his finger, which alludes to Damiel's earlier reference to 'the line of a neck'. In the final moments of his angels' existence, similarly, he grasps the stone that he took from Marion's caravan in his hand. He looks forward to being able to sense the weight and texture of the stone, and not just carry its image.

The figure of Peter Falk, who plays himself, is a second source of temptation for Damiel. Himself an ex-angel, Falk can sense Damiel's presence and addresses him at a snack booth. He extols the merits of everyday sensations enjoyed by humans such as coffee-drinking, cigarette-smoking and hand-rubbing on a cold day. These are then among the first actions Damiel performs after becoming human.

But Falk inspires Damiel in another way, in a more direct parallel to cinema: Falk is a hobby artist and draws portraits of the actors he works with on the set of a war movie being filmed in Berlin – the reason for his presence in the city. When he first senses and addresses Damiel, he describes how, in drawing, a dark line and a light line together make 'a good line'. Light and dark – or light and shadow – being

FIGURE 18 *Wings of Desire* (© 1987, Road Movies Filmproduktion GmbH)

the sole component of the projected cinematic image, has a strong thematic presence in other films: Robert and Bruno's silhouetted mime performance at the school in *Kings of the Road*, and the painter in *The State of Things*, who locates the essence of physical appearance in the contrasts and contradictions between light and dark: 'in nature everything's just lights and darks ... That's what gives it form.' What the artist says of painting is perhaps more a feature of filmic and photographic images, due to the technical procedures involved in their production, particularly if manipulation is excluded from this process. As an ex-angel, Falk is able, literally, to make a mark with his drawing, which is another aspect in which Falk, the human, differs from Damiel, the angel. Just as Damiel has no access to the physical world, his activities are in vain since he has no audience. If Damiel is invisible to most humans, then he – possessor and purveyor of a pure, unmanipulated vision – is unable to make a mark amongst them. Seen this way, the sequence is a further illustration of Damiel's and Wenders' perceived impotence as 'guardians of the sacred image'. In a library sequence involving a pencil – an instrument of inscription – the notes to the script of *Wings of Desire* suggest that Damiel feels this impotence as a physical or emotional pain: 'Damiel's hand comes into view and reaches for a white pencil on the desk. The "actual" pencil remains on the desk, Damiel can only pick up its "likeness".'[61] Shortly afterwards: 'Damiel places the pencil in his lap. He is overcome by a pain (maybe because he could not 'really' pick up the pencil) and he holds onto the balustrade behind him.'[62] Both figures – Marion and Falk – are cast as characters whose activities entice Damiel into his decision to surrender his armour and become a human. Maybe the most significant aspect of their characterisation in this sense is that both figures – the artist and real-life actor Peter Falk, and the trapeze-artist Marion – work with their bodies, and both are able to make a mark amongst their audiences.

A simple but very calculated form of suture is at work throughout *Wings of Desire* that has implications for the development of the narrative as well as for the exploitation of the film image itself as an instrument for viewer manipulation. Like conventional forms of suture, it is based on the alignment and emotional interweaving of audience identification with one of the main protagonists – in this case, Damiel.

Though it can be argued that, as Damiel is unfamiliar with human emotions, it is impossible for the spectator to identify with him on an emotional level merely through the presentation of events from Damiel's subjective point of view, the regular alternation between subjective and objective/independent camera – especially during the first minutes of the film – encourages the development of an independent spectator position towards the situation of the angel as understood in terms of human emotions: the independent point of view distances the spectator from the angel at regular intervals, except when it constitutes a part of a conventional shot/reverse-shot mechanism, which has the function of reinforcing the spectator's identification with Damiel's point of view. This means that the emotions that develop independently within the spectator are separate to those experienced by the angel, though the calculated manipulation of audience point of view ensures that they do, at times, coincide. This is, for instance, a condition necessary for the development in the spectator of sexual desire in connection with the figure of Marion – which Damiel logically cannot experience – in parallel to the angel's actual emotions: desire for experience of the physical world, which Marion represents for him, and which the spectator logically cannot experience. The trigger for the parallel development of different emotions in both angel and spectator is Marion.

Damiel is dissatisfied with his inability to engage in the world of physical existence. Similarly, the fragmentary nature of the audio and visual information available to the spectator ensures the development of a comparable feeling of dissatisfaction at being unable to detect significance in the scraps of information offered in the form of the angel's perception. While the angel begins to show signs of frustration due to his impotence regarding his exclusion from events, the spectator's frustration is based on a similar impotence stemming from the lack of a logical sequence of events, or of recognisable signs of a story – for instance through psychological motivation – during the first half of the film that could allow him to master and make sense of the developments on the screen. Where a desire for increased subjective relevance wells up in the angel, the spectator develops a subjective desire for relevance in the sequence of events on the screen. Because the hero confesses his impotence, and because he is a fantasy figure, identification with him is out of the question: it is rather the case that the spectator, distanced from the main character by the absence of a coherent sequence to the events, develops an independent point of view, to identify, that is, with himself, and with a personal point of view regarding the visual and audio information on the cinema screen. The spectator is, more or less, left to his own devices, and hopes the events on the screen will soon gain coherence. The activity of looking for some kind of relevance is thus shared by both Damiel and the spectator, though each has different motives for his search.

During this part of the film, there are three events that offer the spectator a semblance of coherence, and so function to hold his/her attention: the revelation of Damiel's dissatisfaction and his desire to change his situation in his two meetings with Cassiel; the introduction of the familiar film and television star Peter Falk; and the introduction of the figure of Marion, whose inner monologue we follow for a longer period than that of any other figure and who thus gains significance for the spectator because we can make sense of her thinking. Marion's characterisation through her inner monologue and the notes to the script express the nature of her link with Damiel. As a circus angel, whose role is defined in the image she presents to an audience, Marion is linked to the world of objects, of physical matter, from which Damiel is excluded. Her occupation lends her the fictional role of angel/show girl that seems to give her strength and courage. With the announcement that the circus where she works is to close down for the year due to lack of money, the fictional persona of angel and beauty queen that her trapeze act had allowed her to adopt will be lost. The importance of her assumed identity is clear from her declaration during the circus party that she is 'happy, I have a story, and I'll go on having one'.[63]

Despite this satisfaction, her identity is dependent on forces beyond her control: once the end is spelled out for the circus, she is left alone with her melancholy thoughts, her inner monologue, in which she expresses her desires. It is only her fictional persona that is relevant in her circus role, which, along with her inner thoughts, exposes an incompleteness to her identity:

> Here, I'm a foreigner, yet it's all so familiar. Anyway, I can't get lost, you always end up at the wall. I'll wait for a photo by a machine, it'll come out with a different face. That could be the start of a story ... Anxiety makes me sick. One part of me is anxious, the other part doesn't believe in it. How should I live?[64]

A confusion of identity, considered together with her dependence on a fictional identity, allows for an interpretation of Marion as a development on the figure of Jane in the previous film, *Paris, Texas*. Like Jane, Marion is a performer who works with her body, and is an object of focus for spectators. In *Paris, Texas*, Wenders attempts to redeem the traditional degraded image of women in cinema, setting the conditions for returning a form of identity lost through the commercialisation of images – particularly of women – through his clear statement that this degradation has occurred, and largely at the hands of male film-makers. In *Wings of Desire*, Wenders seems to have been inspired by a figure from German cinematic history – Marlene Dietrich, who appeared as Lola Lola in Josef von Sternberg's *The Blue Angel* (1930) – to again make the same statement, and to suggest more concretely that cinema is capable of effecting this kind of redemption. Apart from the very implicative link with Wenders' angels in the title of von Sternberg's film, and the similarity of the names Marlene and Marion, Dietrich's role as cabaret artist who, in her famous song, is 'in love from head to toe, and nothing else matters', suggests the identification of Marion as Dietrich's modern-day equivalent for whom 'at times, the most important thing is to be beautiful, and nothing else matters'[65] is more than mere speculation. Like Lola Lola, Marion works with her body in a show and becomes the object of male desire. Both figures appear in similarly revealing costumes, and Marion's melancholy is another sign of the relation with her recluse ancestor:

> I waited an eternity to hear a loving word. Then I went abroad. Somebody who'd say 'I love you so much today.' That would be wonderful. I look up and the world emerges before my eyes.[66]

Contrary to Roger Cook's view that Marion assumes a significant role for the spectator much later,[67] it is clear from her interior monologue, which aligns her desire with Damiel's, and the fact that this is the first time Damiel follows one of the many individuals he watches and listens to, that she will be of more consequence to the narrative. Marion's text – 'As a child I wanted to live on an island' – reminds the spectator of the film's opening lines, the beginning of the poem that frames almost the entire film, and which are not only spoken by Damiel but also hand-written by Peter Handke: 'When the child was a child, he'd walk round with his arms hanging down, wishing for the brook to be a river, the river a torrent and this puddle the sea', and is the first time the spectator can forge a link in the disconnectedness of the film's opening fifteen minutes. For the first time, the spectator's desire for coherence aligns itself fully with Damiel's desire for relevance, for it is also the first time that the object of his desire seems within reach, and that his desire equates with earthly concerns that the spectator can recognise.

Another feature of the first sequences with Marion is the sudden use of colour film stock. Where black and white is usually used to signify the presence of an angel, or when the point of view is that of an angel, the colour image signifies the opposite. The choice of colour for Marion's first appearance in *Wings of Desire* solicits a reaction in the spectator in connection with Marion: she appears in the revealing costume she uses for her circus performances, and is without question a beautiful sight after the greyness of everyday Berlin, particularly so in the colourful images. For this reason, her very appearance situates Marion as an iconic object of visual attraction for the spectator, which can be of a sexual nature in a male, heterosexual spectator. At the very least, the use of colour provokes the spectator to question the motives for the sudden change, and to begin attentively looking for explanations and connections. This, and the fact that Marion appears as a pseudo-angel with wings, additionally points towards a connection between her and Damiel, possibly the beginning of a story. In this way, Marion's function as a figure who arouses more curiosity and expectation in the spectator than did the established routine of following Damiel's flight around the city of Berlin takes effect at precisely the same moment as does her function as the main figure to tempt Damiel into surrendering his angelic existence.

Whether or not Dietrich in *The Blue Angel* was a model for the characterisation of Marion, her 'longing for a wave of love' is answered by Damiel's 'loving look' that respects and values the identity of people and objects, has universal knowledge, and is capable of seeing things as they are. Like the semi-pornographic images featuring women in *Paris, Texas*, the disparity between Marion's outer appearance – which she displays as the show girl in *Wings of Desire* – and her inner identity – of which Damiel has knowledge – is the source of her inner conflict. Damiel's (cinema's) exclusive access, through the purity of his perceptional abilities and his knowledge, to Marion's inner self, suggests to the spectator that a union between him and Marion will be one of reciprocals, and that such a union is the desired next step in the film. Such a union can only come about if Damiel takes the decision to surrender his angelic status and become human. The figure of Homer (Curt Bois) provides the key to understanding the nature of such a union, and expresses the hopes Wenders has for cinema as a medium capable of redeeming its relevance.

Kolker and Beicken's assertion that Wenders appears to be on an 'endless, quasi mystical search for the appeasing and accepting father – his real father ... and a search, finally, for the accepting and guiding fathers of world cinema'[68] is supported by Wenders' treatment of the older generation after *Paris, Texas*. But rather than acceptance and appeasement, the search began with a rejection of the fatherly generation: Winter in *Alice in the Cities* might have turned to his family when he ran out of money on the search for Alice's grandmother; his parents are deceased in *Kings of the Road*, the family home is a ruin and Robert Lander refuses his father the opportunity to speak when he sees him, saying 'I always left him in peace. But he never did me'; Travis, through recognising that he had become what his own father had been in *Paris, Texas*, re-acquires language and the ability to act to make good his errors and, with this move, becomes the first of Wenders' characters to directly tackle his relationship with his father through recognition.

After *Paris, Texas*, Wenders' casting of older male figures in his films evolved into the recognition that their knowledge and experience can be instructive, a thing of value and guidance. Wenders describes Homer in *Wings of Desire* as 'neither man nor angel, but both at once, since he's as old as the cinema itself'.[69] Likewise, in *Until the End of the World*, Wenders was interested in Doctor Henry Farber's invention as an instrument that shows 'what he's able to "extract" from the minds of his father and grand-father. That'll be German history from the thirties to the year 2000.'[70] The late Heinz Rühmann plays the part of Konrad in *Far Away, So Close*; Sam Fuller, already present in *The State of Things*, appears again in *The End of Violence*. The ageing musicians that make up the 'Buena Vista Social Club' band in the film of the same name are the latest in this row of ageing male characters to whom Wenders has turned in later years. Bois, Rühmann and Fuller are chattering, reminiscing old men whose tales, whether filmic or oral, have contributed to the documentation of the twentieth century.

The figure of Homer in *Wings of Desire* may be described as the 'divinely inspired voice of narration who incorporates the spirit of human experience from the old epics to the most recent tales of historic events ... the representative and bearer of collective memory, the spirit of history ... the spirit of Berlin'[71] or the 'blind poet, a man of words',[72] but he is also, quite simply, an old man who rambles on about the past. Like the Homer of the classics, Wenders' Homer represents a document that consists of nothing more than the verbal communication of this experience and his views on them, a document that is held in the present. As such, the figure of the old man is, for the first time in Wenders' oeuvre, a figure of authority and invaluable experience. Wenders' own teachers were not those of the Munich Film and Television Academy, rather the old masters of the German cinema, Fritz Lang and F. W. Murnau, or the Hollywood directors Nicholas Ray and John Ford, amongst others, and not least the Japanese director Yazujiro Ozu. Importantly, in 1967, these were all figures who were either already deceased or no longer significantly active. Figures, that is, who had an entire life behind them, an experience which authorises them as witnesses of their time, to qualify them as narrators.

In *Wings of Desire*, we first see Homer on the landing of the Berlin State Library, which also seems to serve as some kind of home or gathering point for the angels. As his name and his monologues would suggest, Homer represents the collective memory of Berlin and the world beyond, the 'immortal poet'[73] who keeps alive the myths of his time passing them down to his listeners through the generations. In interview with Wolfgang Schütte in 1982, Wenders expresses his view that, ever since Homer (the author) stories have served to satisfy a need for coherence in the face of the growing interchangability of visual impressions:

> Telling stories on film aims at recognition from the spectator while the form tries to produce order out of a chaos of impressions. Ever since Homer (whom I'm reading at the moment), mankind has needed stories to learn that coherence is possible. There is a need for connections because human beings don't experience much coherence. Correspondingly, there is an inflationary surge of 'impressions'. I would say that the need for stories is actually greater because you have a narrator ordering experience and suggesting that you can actually take control of your own life. That's what stories do. They confirm your ability to determine the meaning of your own life.[74]

Wenders' first idea had been to cast Bois as an old archangel, but he and Handke were inspired by a reproduction of Rembrandt's Homer that hung on Handke's wall. The picture had been cut into two halves separating Homer from his listeners 'so now he's merely soliloquising'.[75] Thus, in the film, Homer warns:

> Must I give up now? If I do give up, mankind will lose its story-teller. And once mankind has lost its story-teller it will have lost its childhood ... Name me the men, women and children who will look for me, me, their storyteller, their spokesman. For they need me more than anything in the world.

The narrator, in the shape of Homer, has lost his relevance in essentially the same way as Damiel: he too has lost his audience and acknowledges the fact of his listeners' absence and the deficient relationship between them and the texts that have replaced his function: 'With time, those who listened to me became my readers. They no longer sit in a circle. They sit apart now, one knows nothing about the other.'[76] Homer, too, is looking for a new way to continue the 'Epic of Peace. What's wrong with Peace?

What is it that makes its inspiration so undurable, and that makes it so difficult to talk of Peace?'[77] Because of the disaffection of Homer's listeners (due, presumably, to the invention of the book and of printing technology) and the nature of his resulting frustration, he can be understood as a parallel to the film-maker.

Damiel's (cinema's) qualities – his caring glance and his role as eternal observer cite him as the candidate capable of continuing Homer's Epic of Peace. But to reach an audience, to assume Homer's role, he must first become a human. One of the most significant side-effects of Damiel's leap into humanity is the change in the way he experiences time. Indeed, the first consequence of Damiel's fall is the loss of his angelic invulnerability, represented by his armour breastplate, and his passage into a finite temporal dimension. As an angel, able to transcend the time barrier, Damiel experiences time less as a linear flow than as a kind of plane on which all of history is gathered as a single event: the angels 'can move back along an infinite time continuum, viewing past moments as if they were the present'.[78] As a human, Damiel loses his function as contemplative observer and recorder of history, which he bemoans during his first meeting with Cassiel. The term 'eternity/eternal' features three times in his speech, always in a negative context, as do the terms 'spirit(ual)', 'bind', and 'forever'. Conversely, he expresses the desire to say "'Now!' and 'Now!' and 'Now!'" as a positive concept, suggesting that, like Marion, Damiel would like to have boundaries, whether temporal or spatial, to realise his aim of reaching something palpable. This is, indeed, the condition Damiel enters when he becomes human. The new linear temporal dimension he enters thus furnishes Damiel with a structure that orders events sequentially, binding them within a coherent form that has finite boundaries. That these characteristics are also attributes both of story and of Homer's narrative, together with the new capacity to reach an audience, clearly suggests the sentiment that cinema, represented here by Damiel, will only be suited to continuing Homer's Epic of Peace if it is a cinema capable of narration: a narrative cinema. In interview in 1988, Wenders concisely expresses this desire for stories and the structure they can provide in film:

> No, it's not really nostalgia, [storytelling] is almost this new discovery for me. It is one of the most reassuring things. It seems its very basis is that it reassures you that there is a sense to things. Like the fact that children want to hear stories when they go to sleep. I mean, not so much that they want to know this or that, but that they want it as it gives them a security. The story creates a form and the form reassures them so that you can almost tell them any story – which you can actually do. So there is something very powerful in stories, something that gives you security and a sense of identity and meaning. And

it seems to me that this sort of storytelling is disappearing a little bit. Because more and more we seem to be getting them from television and movies, and less and less through books. We're confronted with all these films and images and all that, so it seems that storytelling in that old sense, it's not becoming a lost art, but it's getting less important. And the stories we're being fed with mostly in television and film seem just to pretend being stories. Very often they try to act as if they were stories and are really just pure form, and behind there is just a lot of baloney and noise, especially in most of the films made for young people today that only seem to work if there's a lot of action and violence. That has almost replaced an old story structure, so in that sense you're right there is a nostalgia for stories, for real stories and for an epic feeling of a story.[79]

In *Wings of Desire* Wenders reinvigorates his valuation of cinema's ability to present an image of physical reality 'photographically', because 'no other language is as capable of addressing itself to the physical reality of things'.[80] The dominant trend in commercial cinema that Wenders perceives to consist only of pure form and little content except for highlights, action, violence and sensations can, he states in this film, be countered if the spectator once again learns that mere existence is a real and worthwhile sensation. Damiel's caring glance and simple observation of the environment represents such attentiveness and, as such, is cited as a key to accessing the secret of existence described in Handke's text.[81] At the same time, Wenders seeks a form for the presentation of his images, which he hopes will satisfy audience demand for coherence in their cinematic experience.

More so than in *Paris, Texas*, *Wings of Desire* remains a fragmentary collection of impressions, without ever seeking to develop a story out of these. The film's episodic structure is linked only by the figure of Damiel, and the forward movement of the minimalistic plot is based on the development and realisation of his desires, which holds the film together. Each stage of this development, each episode, is introduced anew with the reiteration of Damiel's poem beginning with 'When the child was a child...'. If the development of the plot has any other line to follow, it is an imaginary one that runs between Damiel's companion, Cassiel, a figure who remains in the background and from whom Damiel wants to distance himself, and Marion, who appears up front in the circus ring, and towards whom Damiel wants to move. The 'love story' is used purely as a frame, a recognisable plot element that is there only to satisfy the demands of the spectator for story. With the fulfilment of his desire to become human, Damiel imports his childlike vision – the camera-eye – into life with him, and his visual impressions gain a new sequential, logical order, as opposed to the previous arbitrariness of his impressions. The conclusion for Wenders is thus less a discovery of story as a positive force than many critics would like to see in this film:[82] it is merely a more resolute re-affirmation of his consistently held position regarding the role of stories, bluntly expressed by the director Friedrich in *The State of Things*: 'stories only exist in stories (whereas life goes by without the need to turn it into stories)'.

The Million Dollar Hotel

The movie camera as an angel, purveyor of a childlike vision that is accepting and unopinionated; that represents a kind of vision that Wenders wishes for his films. This is one aspect that makes his latest feature film, *The Million Dollar Hotel*, fit in so well with the rest of his work, despite the fact that it also represents a step into new territory, new experimentation with the storytelling capabilities of film. New in this film is above all the stronger characterisation than usual of the supporting actors and actresses, and the diegetical space: the film almost never leaves the confines of the hotel of the film's title.

Opening the Berlin Film Festival in 2000, *The Million Dollar Hotel* largely failed to meet the expectations of the international press. Once again, criticism focused mainly on the film's narrative weaknesses: while *Screen International*'s Derek Malcolm found the film's narrative drive 'too weak to sustain its 122 minutes length',[83] Merten Worthmann of the leading German weekly *Die Zeit* found the fragmentary nature of the narrative to be the film's main problem: 'The individual plot elements and the many characters continually crash into one another, and everything the story is supposed to say, but can't quite seem to be able to show, is dubbed in later in a scarcely disguised moral-of-the-story voice-over.'[84] A full year later, Elvis Mitchell of *The New York Times* adds weight to these critiques, remarking that the film 'wafts across the screen like ashes from a dying fire: it lacks the decisive logic and Point A to Point B payoff that is normally associated with Mel Gibson movies'.[85] *Variety.com*, in contrast, is intrigued by the plot but describes the film as a 'tough sell' and a 'commercial non-starter'.[86]

The same critics are almost as united in praising the images of the film as they are in bemoaning its narrative. What is interesting about this situation is that it would seem to confirm Wenders' continuing bid to promote the photographic image and a certain visual mode, and to have images dominate over narrative in film. For Wenders, therefore, the critical response may just have been what he was hoping for, a confirmation of success in the context of his filmic investigation of the relationship between image and story. Whether or not the film is considered 'good' or 'watchable' or, indeed, a 'commercial non-starter' is an entirely different question. Interesting is also that commercial images and commercially abused images, as well as the artificial nature of stories, is, once again, just what the film is about.

The Million Dollar Hotel and the themes it develops are braced within the structure of a more present than usual framework story that has a much more 'dominant' presence than in any of the director's previous films. Israel (Izzy) Goldkiss (Tim Roth), a resident of the Los Angeles hotel for the down-and-out, falls to his death from the rooftop of the hotel. It does not become clear until the end of the film whether it was an accident, suicide or murder. Ruthless FBI Special Agent Skinner (Mel Gibson) is hired by the dead man's father, a media mogul and owner of a commercial television company, to investigate his son's death, but he does not get anywhere because all the hotel residents who might have useful information are, in some way, mad and absorbed in their own preoccupations.

Izzy's best friend is the good-hearted, but retarded, Tom Tom (Jeremy Davies). Skinner recognises that he can take advantage of Tom Tom's good nature to discover the identity of the murderer, and has Geronimo (Jimmy Smits), another of the hotel residents, arrested in order to force the truth out of Tom Tom. To save Geronimo from prison, Tom Tom agrees to the recording on video of his confession to the crime, which is then aired on television. When the police come to arrest him, he himself jumps from the roof, which takes the film back to the images it began with.

Two other narrative strands are built into this frame. The first involves the figure of Eloise (Milla Jovovich). Eloise was raped by Izzy – or, at least, Tom Tom, who is in love with her, understands this to have happened. This, we discover, is why he allowed Izzy to jump to his death from the roof after initially trying to stop him. The second narrative strand involves a scam by the hotel residents to take advantage of the public interest in Izzy's death by passing Geronimo's tar paintings off as having been painted by Izzy, in order to sell them at a profit.

Unlike in all the previous films, the flight in and out of the diegesis at the beginning and end of *The Million Dollar Hotel* does not give the impression that one is witnessing an episode in the daily life of the film's protagonists. This was surely the intention, but the framework story is much too strong, too present, too fast-paced and, in a way, too closed for this strategy to be as effective as in, for example, *Alice in the Cities*, *Wrong Movement*, and even *The End of Violence*.[87] The first sequence after the flight into the film therefore detracts attention from the first frames, becoming the real beginning of the film, especially because, from the dramaturgical point of view, Tom Tom's suicide is a clear highlight. Two attributes of the suicide sequence in particular heighten its dramatic force: Tom Tom, the suicidal main protagonist, waves and smiles at an unseen person (or maybe at the camera) in the very moment at which he is putting an end to his life – a surreal image that adds to the speculation surrounding his motives; secondly, how the film will end becomes clear immediately after Tom Tom jumps, and we know that his voice-over commentary is that of a dead character. The voice-over itself, too, contributes to narrative development as, from the beginning, it introduces many of the narrative factors at play, and imitates a story that is being told from the beginning:

> I guess you could say my life only really started about two weeks ago. That's when I lost my best friend, Izzy, and found Eloise. Oh, Eloise! She was something to live for, and I guess that means something to die for.

The fact that the end of the story is known at the beginning means that spectator activity is diverted away from waiting for the story to end. Instead, the mystery generated by the fact and the nature of the suicide encourages the spectator to slip into the role of a detective and to search for clues: how and why did it come to this?

As if to confirm that this is expected of the spectator, Wenders' detective, in the form of Mel Gibson, never actually discovers any information regarding the murder mystery. Despite this, Skinner is the primary agent of forward narrative movement. He is introduced as a comedy figure, a parody of a detective, which softens the extremely ruthless impression that he initially makes. He would rather be on holiday with his lover, but is too dedicated an agent to leave the case before it is wrapped up. Skinner's regular telephonic dialogues with his lover, ending with the break up of the relationship, are part of the comic aspect of his characterisation, as is the banana skin he almost steps on as he gets out of his car, which alludes to his name, 'Skinner', and suggests from his first appearance that he will get nowhere. Despite the strength of Skinner's characterisation and his heavy presence, his role as chief investigator in this case is, above all, a pretext for the camera to move from room to room through the hotel, for the spectator to get to know all its inhabitants. This activity is what moves the narrative on.

By the end of the first hour of the film three narrative strands have evolved that progress simultaneously: the murder mystery continues, though it is essentially reduced to Skinner's appearances; the art scam, which develops from an initiative by the hotel residents to take advantage of the media interest in the apparent murder of a billionaire tycoon's dropout son to sell Geronimo's paintings; and the love story that develops between Tom Tom and Eloise. In contrast to the art scam, this last narrative

FIGURE 19 *The Million Dollar Hotel* (© 1999, Road Movies Filmproduktion GmbH)

strand is only linked to the murder mystery through Skinner, who, hoping to derive information by bugging Tom Tom's room, contrives together with Eloise to get Tom Tom to talk to her in the privacy of his own room. Effectively, Skinner's investigations make the love story possible.

As complex and, from the point of view of the narrative elements that are introduced, as cinematically attractive as this web of diverse intrigues may seem to be, they mainly serve to introduce and develop the film's chief thematic motif in unison: the discourse on commercial and commercialised images, in which Wenders falls back on the same strategies of allusion that he employs, above all, in *The State of Things*, *Paris, Texas*, and *Wings of Desire*.

The murder mystery plays the two similar but contrasting figures of Skinner and Stanley Goldkiss (Harris Yulin) against one another. Their first meeting in a car driving through the streets of Los Angeles at night recalls Friedrich and Gordon's night-time drive through the same city in *The State of Things* eighteen years earlier. Where Gordon insisted that 'a film without a story is like a house without walls', here, Goldkiss also appears to be insisting on the fabrication of a story that will satisfy the media's interest in his son's death. By satisfy, Goldkiss means a story that diverts attention away from the theory that it was a case of suicide – for Goldkiss the Jew, the ultimate in shame, and for Goldkiss the prominent media man, a possible media circus that could implicate him as the cause of the suicide. In each case, Goldkiss is primarily concerned with his reputation, less with the actual circumstances surrounding his son's death:

> I don't know whether my son was killed to get at me, but I know that his death has great entertainment potential. He came from money and power, lived with bums and Indians ... died mysteriously ... Easy headlines! A media circus.

Goldkiss speaks from experience. He readily admits to Skinner, by way of explanation, that his own company is active in fabricating facts to suit the buyers' market. The victim of this practice, Wenders wants to express in this sequence, is truth. To Skinner's offer of getting at the truth behind the death, Goldkiss laughs and cynically replies:

> Truth? My people decide the truth in over sixty countries every morning, and in each one it's different. The truth is the explanation that most people want to buy. And what my rivals want to buy is any piece of shit they can get on me to flush me down the toilet ... This is Hollywood, my boy. They invented the [information] game. They don't need much here. One ounce of shit and they make a shit soufflé!

This discussion between a character who is only satisfied with the truth, and a character who specialises in the fabrication of commercially viable stories which are then presented as the truth, is the most literal filmic expression yet of Wenders' conviction that stories inherently signify the negation or degradation of truth. That the medium in question is television, and the location is, once again, Los Angeles and Hollywood, completes Wenders' reaffirmation in this film that image production in a commercially oriented production environment involves the manipulation of truth in the image, especially when the images in question are subordinated to the role of supporting a dominant story; commercial pressure is the underlying cause for this type of image degradation, Wenders suggests. His criticism, especially of television ('optical toxin'), is more bluntly expressed in *The Million Dollar Hotel* than in earlier films in which, for example, merely showing a television with a blank screen, or playing on the restrictions of televisual framing, sufficed. Television is omnipresent in this film as a sort of aggressively self-assertive authority on fact and reality. The characters inhabiting the hotel accept it as such, and seem to take advantage of this presumed status. In fact, however, they take advantage of the medium's obvious drawbacks, most notably, of the commercial pressures that dictate its content. The art scam is not merely a concoction of the hotel residents. It is an opportunistic attempt at capitalising on the inaccurate, sensationalistic reporting practices that lead the television company 'Channel 6 News' (Goldkiss's main competitor), which obviously senses that bending the facts just a little would result in the creation of a news sensation, to falsely report that the dead Izzy was the painter of Geronimo's paintings. Here again, the facts – the truth – fall victim to commercial pressures. Geronimo's interview, in which he in fact speaks about his paintings, how they express the loss of the Indian culture, is cut at a decisive moment, which makes it sound like Izzy was the painter:

GERONIMO: … lost forever, without a trace …
[CUT]
GERONIMO: … like Izzy!

Additionally, the aesthetic limitations of television are made obvious in the interview sequence, as the cameraman recording the interview explains to Tom Tom that '[TV] magnifies everything. He shouldn't be making big gestures. He's moving his hands all over the place!' Such images are, of course, those for which cinema is perfectly suited to record and show; a larger, wider image that captures the context – the reality of the residents' predicament – which the small, narrow television image has to leave outside the frame. To summarise the sensation, the television moderator closes the story of Izzy's death with the words: '… who died in poverty without selling a single painting', and a close-up on the moderator's lips as she pronounces the word 'selling'.

The art scam ends with an art dealer bluntly and cynically explaining that his judgement often makes art what it is – 'therefore, the artist is often merely the painter, and the dealer is actually the artist!' – and, resulting from Skinner's only investigative success in the film, the tar paintings turn out to have been painted over actual paintings stolen from an art gallery. Wenders' statement in these sequences is a no less blunt and cynical comment on the commercial pressures that inform international cinema, especially bearing in mind the film's location, in close proximity to Hollywood's dream factories, and Wenders' experience working there on Coppola's *Hammett* between 1977 and 1982.

These pressures have their victims in the film, the main protagonists Eloise and Tom Tom. Though Eloise's surname is Ash, Tom Tom appears to refer to her as 'Miss Brooks' in one of the several scenes in which he imitates Skinner's verbal articulation and posture. This, and several other aspects of her characterisation would point to

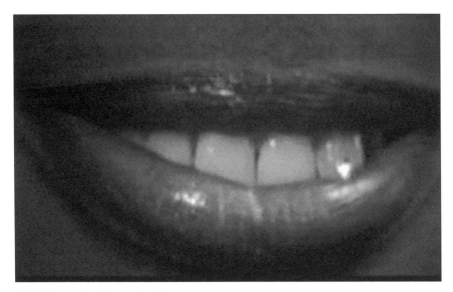

FIGURE 20 *The Million Dollar Hotel* (© 1999, Road Movies Filmproduktion GmbH)

the possibility that, here, Wenders is alluding to the American actress Louise Brooks, who starred in the role of Lulu in G. W. Pabst's film *Pandora's Box* (1929). Lulu, too, makes her living and important connections as a high-class prostitute, ending up in a London doss-house, where she is killed by Jack the Ripper. The allusion to a screen figure is strengthened by Tom Tom's description of Eloise as moving 'like a shadow, you could almost see right through her', and Izzy's claim that 'she's not even there' suggests that Eloise only exists as her screen image. If these parallels are intentional, it would place Eloise in the same family of those female characters in Wenders' movies, such as Jane in *Paris, Texas* and Marion (Marlene Dietrich/Lola Lola) in *Wings of Desire*, who, representing commercially abused and degraded images in general, seek to break out of their existence as no more than an image. As in these two cases, the identity of the image subject, in this case Eloise, falls victim to the male obsession with a commercialised erotic image of women (the area around the hotel, where Eloise wanders by night, is teeming with pornographic cinemas showing '*peliculas calientes*' (or 'hot movies')), to which Wenders' description of her character in an interview as a kind of sleeping beauty, 'asleep to herself and the world', attests.[88]

Tom Tom is clearly the victim of the commercial pressures informing image production in the film: he is a great fan of television, seeming to consider an appearance in its images as the ultimate goal in life, a confirmation of existence, of having 'made it'. His televised confession to the murder of his best friend is therefore simultaneously a dream come true for him, and, because of his naïveté, his blind

FIGURE 21 *The Million Dollar Hotel* (© 1999, Road Movies Filmproduktion GmbH)

trust in a media institution he so admires, it also seals his fate, leading him to his death shortly afterwards. Ironically, Tom Tom confesses, and dies, to save a friend, Geronimo, from his unjust imprisonment for the murder. The thread linking these circumstances, and also the murder mystery involving Skinner, is a concept of the truth put forward by the film: Skinner is the only character who is looking for the truth, and never finds it, while it is television that constantly falsifies the truth of events at an institutional level, and presents its findings as the truth. Television more than gets in the way of truth: it bends the truth into something suiting its commercial purposes. In the end, it no longer really matters that Tom Tom's lie, his confession to the murder, is so readily accepted by the Channel 6 News programme: the damage was done even before the film began, with all the characters having already become outcasts of the Hollywood-propagated 'American Dream'. It is, essentially, commercial images that determine the course of events in this film, despite Skinner's attempts at steering his suspects into his trap. Only the television company gets what it wants in the end. When confronted with the daily existence of the hotel residents, forgotten and living on the edges of society, television's habitual fabrication of stories, of the truth, as it is stated in *The Million Dollar Hotel*, reminds one again of the director Friedrich's clash with his Hollywood producer in *The State of Things*.

As is the case in all of the previously discussed films, here, again, it is not the outcome of the story that is important in the end. Though, at times, narrative progress is fast-paced and seemingly determined, it does not lead to the promised resolving of the foregrounded murder mystery, despite the fact that we follow a detective whose job it is to find a murderer. Any feeling that there is still some truth to be discovered regarding the identity of the murderer evaporates completely when Tom Tom simply states what happened just before he jumps from the roof of the hotel, which wrenches the pleasurable speculative activity of working this out for themselves from the hands of the spectators at the same time as underlining the meaninglessness of this information in the film's context: 'So now you know!' Tom Tom finishes. Neither can we eagerly await the end of any story, because this was already served up to us at the very beginning of the film. Clearly, with the foregrounded story already 'wrapped up' by the circular narrative structure, there is not much more for the spectator to do other than to observe the images, the characters, and listen to the music. In contrast to the depicted world of commercialised images, which uses images as supporting evidence for fabricated stories, *The Million Dollar Hotel* attempts to show what lies beyond the American Dream, a story that is usually ignored, within the frame of an elaborate fiction.

Lisbon Story

As we can see from the analysis of the previous films, Wenders exploits the film image as the primary information-bearing device because, being a photographic reproduction of reality, it takes its raw material from a given physical environment in order to emphasise the presence of that environment or of individual objects within it: 'a skin-to-skin contact of sensitive *pellicula* [celluloid] and the corpus of reality'.[89] Story, on the other hand, seldom has more importance in Wenders' films than for the provision of a frame in which the images appear. A traditional filmic story, as it does not originate from the act of recording the existence of visual reality, presents a constructed rendition of space, related in a time-frame that is also artificial. Though a film-maker might attempt, through suture, to convince the spectator of the authenticity of a story, Wenders refuses to accept the information offered by a story as a comparatively authoritative account of events, and correspondingly places the responsibility to transmit information of this kind on the image.

That a story must be plucked from a physical environment if it is not to manipulate the images that convey it, meaning that images must not be forced into telling a story, is a fundamental condition that, for Wenders, makes the difference between an authentic and a degraded image.[90] In an interview with Peter Jansen in 1989, Wenders expresses his belief that only when each image has something to say in itself does one have the right to place it in conjunction with others to form a whole.[91] Although Wenders was speaking about images, the same is true of his position on film sound.

Lisbon Story explores the potential in film for sound to act in similar ways as the film image. In the introduction to the script, Wenders refers to the pressures which he perceives to threaten the integrity and expressive force of images, and their resulting degradation, to specify his motives for making the film: 'We live in a time when the visible aspect is so predominant that sometimes words, sounds, and music are able to strengthen images, to sustain them. The aim of this film is to show that sounds can help things to be seen differently.'[92]

One technique Wenders employs to promote the expressive force of sound, and which can be evidenced not only in *Lisbon Story*, but in all of his films, is a relative autonomy of the soundtrack from the image. In this, Wenders' position is a development on the film-ideological debate among the Soviet directors Sergei Eisenstein, Vsevolod Pudovkin and Grigori Alexandrov in 1928, in which they advocate a contrapuntal use of sound in film, maintaining that sound should operate as a separate montage element instead of simply underlining the image.

> Sound, treated as a new montage element (as a factor divorced from the visual image), will inevitably introduce new means of enormous power to the expression and solution of the most complicated tasks that now oppress us with the impossibility of overcoming them by means of an imperfect film method, working only with visual images.[93]

Walter Ruttmann was contemporaneously following a similar line to the Soviets. Writing in the *Reichsfilmblatt* in September 1928, Ruttmann described a possible future role for sound in film of simply supporting the image as a fundamental error:

> It's not the job of sound film to free the tongue of the silent cinema ... Counterpoint, optical-acoustic counterpoint must become the basis of all sound-filmic creation. The rivalry between image and sound, their interplay, their occasional fusion, that undoes itself again only to lead to a new rivalry – these are the possibilities.[94]

Such separation of sound from image, and the resulting autonomy that the film sound enjoys, can potentiate an inversion of the traditional subordination of sound to image in film, a concept sustained by Béla Balázs and, more recently, by John Belton. A noise, writes Balázs, sounds differently if it is perceived together with its physiognomy, its image. The image typically dominates over sound in terms of its ability to convince the listener/spectator of the authenticity of the object perceived due, according to Balázs, to sound's status as an attribute of the image.[95] If the source of a sound is not visible, the listener seeks an image that corresponds to the sound with which to associate it. When the source of the sound becomes visible, the listener transcends initial doubts caused by the lack of a corresponding image, testing the sound and image together against reality. A sound alone, Belton agrees, lacks "'objectivity" (thus authenticity) not only because it is invisible but because it is an attribute and is thus incomplete in itself. Sound achieves authenticity only as a consequence of its submission to tests imposed upon it by other senses – primarily by sight.[96]

Regarded as an element separate from the image, Wenders rarely uses sound simply to accompany the image unless it is ambient sound or, significantly, music.[97] Rarely are sounds synchronised with the images simply to increase the impression and illusion of presence. Instead, Wenders insists that sound is more articulate than just acting as an alibi for the image. The image may say one thing, but the sound can say another, or, can say something else about the subject of the image. In allowing the soundtracks of his films a significant degree of autonomy from the images, Wenders hopes that sounds will be heard and respected in their own right, so contributing to the amount and quality of the information his films can offer to the spectators.

One episode of *Kings of the Road* illustrates this complete separation of sound and image within a single sequence for the communication of information. Robert discovers a grieving man in a grain silo and invites him to enter the lorry he and Bruno are travelling in. Sitting down, he tells Robert the story of how the accident occurred, that he suspects suicide and implicates himself as the cause of his wife's death. Inter-cut into this sequence are shots of Bruno in the cab of the lorry, who overhears the man's story. When the man has finished, Bruno quietly leaves to inspect the crash scene. He opens the door of the car and closely examines the driver's seat where, presumably, the man's wife had died earlier the same day. Here, the soundtrack conveys information about the accident and the man's reactions, his psychological state, through his oral communication of the incident to Robert. Already with an image of the scene in our minds, the camera shows us the images of the crash scene through Bruno's eyes, and his psychological reactions to what he sees and what he has heard through the wall of his truck. The images are shown separately from, and later than, the soundtrack which informs the spectator of events. The fact that the images, which ought to correspond to the man's story, are seen through the filter of Bruno's vision and understanding means that the sequence of images gains a new dimension through the use of sound. We see two different reactions to the same event, a subjective and an objective reaction.

This non-synchronic use of sound has the effect of abstracting the simple fact of the occurrence of the accident, making the scene one of many facets, not just the image with an accompanying soundtrack. The sound tells one man's story of the accident, while the image shows another's experience of the same event. Blurring the point of view here significantly adds to and enriches the narrative information conveyed than would be the case if sound and image were synchronised, acting in unison.

A second such example is the film *Wings of Desire*. Of the first sixty minutes of the film, about 90 per cent of verbal communication consists of the inner monologues of the many figures that appear before the camera. Thereafter, the inner monologues make up about 50 per cent of verbal communication. This offers the spectator information about the inner states of the respective figures, while the image shows us these figures and their physical environment: the city of Berlin. Here, the inner monologues of the Berliners tell us one thing separate from, but related to, the information conveyed by the images, just as the man's story in *Kings of the Road* offers his mental and verbal reaction to an event later shown in images. But, in each case, the sound informs us of a psychological condition, while the image provides visual information about the figures concerned and their physical environment. The audience is shown, and is offered reactions to what it is shown, through the soundtrack, which simultaneously encourages the formation in the spectator of an independent point of view regarding the events shown. The soundtrack helps life in Berlin to be seen and understood differently from the picture offered by the images of the city alone. The texts spoken by the many figures as inner monologues could well exist independently and must be closely listened to. Rather than contributing to the completeness of the film's images, Handke's texts add information on a level parallel to the information offered by the image,[98] and must be listened to as closely as the image is scrutinised in order to receive all the narrative information the film has to offer.

This use of sound has significance for the modern cinematic experience, for it aims to maximise the amount of information the spectator receives. If sound is synchronised – a car drives past and you hear the noise of its engine, the tyres, and so on, the picture is so completely empirical that the sound is, as much as possible, invisible: it is beyond doubt that it is generated by the subject of the image. The sound, in this case, underlines the image, which contributes only to the concreteness of the image. It is an attribute of the subject of the image. The soundtracks mentioned above in connection with *Kings of the Road* and *Wings of Desire* do not have directly corresponding images. Sound and image form a kind of audio-visual collage. The two levels only meet in that they complement one another. When the sound heard together with an image is not generated by the subject of the image, then the sound can instead be used to add additional information.

This affects the process of storytelling in the following ways: because no coherent story is offered by the film the audience is discouraged from identifying with any character who controls the development of events. Character identification is not a question in either of the two scenes above. A traditional story, of the type we would expect in dominant cinema, would, conversely, present the given accounts of events as the only accounts possible, in order that the audience does not lose the thread of the story, and that the story can near its conclusion. Here, however, the audience is made conscious of the fact that the account of events shown is *an* account instead of *the* account. This is brought about through the use of distancing devices that discourage character identification, through the breaking-down of the illusion of reality. This, in turn, is achieved through the division of sound and image, along with their elevation to the primary information-bearing devices in the film.

The inversion of the dominance of image over sound increases the relevance of film sound as an independently working expressive device, and overturns Belton's claim that sounds 'lack objectivity'. The idea of conferring a greater responsibility on sound as an information carrier seems to have interested Wenders from the very beginning, during his days as a film critic. Almost without exception, he constantly and repeatedly links his emotions with the music in a film rather than with the film itself, or he finds music which expresses what he wants to say about an unconnected film. His critique of *Easy Rider* is a good example of this early trend:

> In *Easy Rider* the film images have become superfluous already, because they only illustrate the music, rather than the other way round. They are merely the relics of a visual sense that's far more current in music than in pictures, which are no more than a cold and exhausted shadow of films that could sustain their own beauty or nostalgia or pathos.[99]

Wenders attempts the same inversion of the sound/image balance in one of his early films, *3 American LPs*. Here, he contrasts the flat images of the Munich suburbs with contemporary American rock music in the soundtrack, while he and Peter Handke talk about the music that is playing. Their conversation focuses on the effect of the music on the images, and how American rock music is suited to Wenders' utopian idea of cinema because it is also 'a visible music that's visible and audible at the same time. That's why you really can describe it as film music.' Music accentuates the visible here, allowing the visual world to appear differently. The music is as 'visible' as the images, but the images convey a sense of emptiness, sombreness, and the music is full of utopian emotive force. The images seem either randomly put together or chosen for the music; the music and the commentary are the only things that bind together the fragmentary atmosphere in the images. We do not know whether the music is there for the images or the other way around. Just as in the other early films, the images in *3 American LPs* are purely contemplative, and therefore do not attempt to carry meaning, but to show. The combination with American rock music, then, fills the empty images with a contrasting mood that makes the conditions of life in the Munich suburbs transparent. Here, as in *Kings of the Road*, the soundtrack contributes to the complete picture that Wenders' film presents us because it adds a mood or information of a different kind to that offered in the images of the film. The main contribution of the music in *3 American LPs*, that Wenders identifies in the commentary, is 'emotion': the music is 'more vivid', providing exactly that which Wenders feels is missing in the images and, perhaps, in his experience of the Munich suburbs.

In *Lisbon Story* Wenders effectively challenges Balàzs's position regarding the subordination of sound to image, by implicitly emphasising the latter's distinction between the chaotic noises of everyday life, and the sound that is isolated from the 'chaos of shapeless noise by accepting it as expression, significance and meaning.'[100] The very same Philip Winter from *Alice in the Cities* returns as a sound technician in *Lisbon Story*. Called to Lisbon by a friend who needs help with the soundtrack of his film, it is Winter's job in Lisbon to explore the city looking not for the various sights, but into its acoustic landscape in search of the sounds that the city generates.

One of Winter's first discoveries is Madredeus, the Portuguese *fado* group that features in the film as they are recording the song '*Ainda*'. As Teresa, the vocalist, sings, Winter watches her shadow, cast on the wall in a pool of white light. In the first place, here, such a degree of separation is achieved between sound and image that the usual subordination of sound is inverted. The image of Teresa's shadow (a negative image because it is a shadow) seems almost like an attribute of the music, which contrasts with sound's more usual status as an attribute of the image. The individual band members are indistinguishable in the dark blue light of the recording studio, but the sound rings crisply and clearly.

Secondly, the fact that Wenders uses his band both diegetically and non-diegetically in *Lisbon Story* (Madredeus are seen performing live, recording the music for both Friedrich's and Wenders' films) contributes to the autonomy of the music soundtrack. They are presented as a group of musicians who have a unity and an existence outside the context of the film, which one would normally expect from a documentary, rather than from a feature film. Their music illustrates the city, not the images of the film.

FIGURE 22   *Lisbon Story*   (© 1994, Road Movies Filmproduktion GmbH)

Two out of the four songs they perform in the film are about Lisbon: *Tejo*, the name of the city's river,[101] and *Alfama*, the ancient district where Friedrich, Winter's friend, lives. In this way, the film's music adds expression, significance and meaning to the film, rather than to the images. The songs are neither cut nor dissolved when they finish, but are respected as pieces. The following evening, one of the band's guitarists hands Winter the digital audio cassette containing the soundtrack for both Wenders' and Friedrich's films. The soundtrack of the film is concretely seen, here, to be a physically separate entity to the film. The music, because it appears in its own right rather than functioning to underline the film's images, can be considered to bring an 'extra' quality to the film. This goes both for Friedrich's and for Wenders' film, *Lisbon Story*, for which the band provides the same music.

Beyond the use of music in *Lisbon Story*, the sounds Winter records and improvises in Lisbon are also thematically dealt with in a way that makes their physical separation from the image apparent. The question of sound's relation with images and stories is dealt with mainly in Winter's encounters with the children who live in Lisbon's ancient quarters. The first to appear is Ze who, at fourteen years, is the oldest of the tribe of children. Expecting to find sounds amongst Winter's equipment, Ze opens one of the cases but complains that there are no sounds. These are just the instruments for making them, but to the child's simplistic understanding it is a question of not yet being able to visualise the sounds. To satisfy Ze's doubt, Winter confirms this point with a word play, using a terminology normally reserved for the visual world, to make reference to the traditional audio-visual order of dominance: 'I'll show you.' A similar example of how the language of vision is used to refer to sound is when Friedrich points out Ricardo to Winter saying, 'Can't you see, he's mute.'

Winter's display of his sound effects is a sequence that reminds us that sound, too, can be a source of charm and wonder in the cinema. He prepares his equipment out of sight of the children and improvises the sounds of a galloping horse, a burning fire, an egg being fried and a lion roaring. He encourages the children to build a story from what they hear, which they do through imaginative visualisation. They are not told what to hear, and make up their own story by visualising in their minds the sounds they are given. The children are free to interpret as they like the sounds that Winter improvises, and are not forced towards a predetermined conclusion by them. The story and images rise out of the sounds themselves, and from within the children's collective imagination. The sounds act only as a trigger provoking imaginative activity. In a similar sequence later, Winter is alone with one of the children, Beta. Both have a set of headphones and listen to the city which neither can see. Again, the child identifies what she hears.

For Wenders, sound possesses an equal potential to present an accurate acoustic, or audio-graphic, image of the physical world as the film image. Allowing sound to realise its full expressive force without necessarily corresponding to a visual referent requires, in film, a significant degree of spatial or temporal separation and autonomy from the image, sometimes even a complete autonomy. That this can go so far as to effect an inversion of sound's status as an attribute of the image is confirmed in the film for Winter by one of the verses he reads by the Portuguese writer/philosopher Fernando Pessoa who, like Winter, works with his eyes closed.: 'In some place on the inside of my eyelids, I see nothing but Lisbon with its houses of many colours ... In broad daylight even the sounds shine.' And: 'I have wanted, like sounds, to live by things and not be theirs ... I listen without looking and so see.'[102]

In turning his microphone on the city of Lisbon, Winter and Wenders perform the very same role of isolating individual sounds from the 'chaos of shapeless noise' that Balázs describes in his writings,[103] sounds that can potentially give rise to an image or initiate a story. Winter's directional microphone 'looks' more carefully, isolating the individual sounds that set this city apart from just any city, and that one would not immediately associate with a corresponding image, but as sounds alone: first, the sound of church bells which, in a catholic country always carry a message of birth, of death, of marriage, or simply a call to mass. They are part of the jumble of noises that every Christian city generates, but only in their absence would they seem suddenly

FIGURE 23 *Lisbon Story* (© 1994, Road Movies Filmproduktion GmbH)

and uncomfortably conspicuous; next, an arguing couple is isolated from the acoustic environment, then the sound of a child singing and the running footsteps and lively, chattering voices of other children on the way to school; finally, we hear the sound of pigeons taking flight – what would a city be without them? Through this activity, Wenders is essentially involving the spectator in the same game as the children earlier: listening to, identifying and respecting sounds that exist in a real physical environment, to which we have gained access via the film *Lisbon Story*. This is a function of film sound that corresponds to that of the image in Wenders' aesthetic.

Due to the several direct references to silent cinema in *Lisbon Story*, it is more than mere speculation to assume a connection between Wenders' application of sound in this film and the conventions of sound in the days before it became a technical reality in film. Although early cinema is referred to as silent, films would almost always be accompanied by live music because it had not yet developed the technology to record sound as part of the production process. Speech was communicated through intertitles. Since the advent of sound, however, it has never again been subject to such a degree of separation from the image. This is true not only in the physical sense, but also in the sense that the music for a film was often unscripted, improvised by the musicians at the performance. For his film *Man with a Movie Camera* (1928), for example, to which Wenders dedicates *Lisbon Story*, Dziga Vertov only gave instructions for the type of music he desired for each sequence. This four-page document was then distributed to three composers engaged by the Sovkino Council of Music for the preparation of orchestral cue-sheets for the first projection in April 1929. Only much later was an official musical script prepared for the film.[104]

In *Lisbon Story*, the direct allusions to the silent era include the use of an aperture to dissolve shots and sequences; and the Portuguese director Manoel de Oliveira imitates Chaplin who, even for a long time after the invention of sound, preferred to work without it. The final slapstick-style sequence, and the use of the old movie camera, further strengthen the link with the silent cinema, but in a very particular way: in the earlier sequence with the children, Winter clasps his headphones onto the old camera as if to furnish it with a hearing capability. Secondly, in the final sequence, Winter and Friedrich roam the streets of Lisbon with the old camera, but unlike Vertov's film, which shares the obsession with trams, Friedrich's film is to have a soundtrack. As much as *Lisbon Story* is a celebration of *Man with a Movie Camera*, which Vertov describes as the 'first film without subtitles, an international film' that, 'with the language of the cinema alone, describes the behaviour of man',[105] Wenders clearly suggests that cinema needs and has benefited from sound without necessarily following the 'line of least resistance' that the Soviets had warned of in their manifesto of 1928, and in which the dominant Hollywood cinema decided to find a safe haven for its images where it still lies today, 'providing a certain "illusion" of talking people, of audible objects, et cetera'.[106]

The allusions to silent cinema in *Lisbon Story* show that sound can function on a much higher level as a tool of expression. But it would be too much to assume that Wenders favours a return to the aesthetics of silent cinema because, as we see in this film, sound can also be a source of creative expression in modern cinema. As such, the deployment of sound in the silent era serves as a source of inspiration regarding the use of sound in modern film. Paradoxically, Wenders implies, sound enjoyed its maximum expressive potential at a time when there was no sound in film, when sound, in the form of a musical accompaniment, was a separate entity from the image. Free of its future role of merely supporting image and story in film, sound functioned independently as a generator of meaning, a carrier of information, a source of expression able to 'depict' physical existence in the same way as the image. This is how sound functions in *Lisbon Story*. The film's story is no more than an instrument, entirely a pretext and completely lacking a plot of any relevance: instead, the film is about the city of Lisbon, which we are shown in images and in sounds that do not compete with one another for dominance, but coexist within the frame of the story.

CONCLUSION

Things have a life of their own,' the gypsy proclaimed with a harsh accent.
'It's simply a matter of waking up their soul.'
Gabriel García Márquez, *One Hundred Years of Solitude*

As becomes clear from his own disclosures on the subject of the cinema as an
institution, Wenders heavily charges cinema and film-makers with important
responsibilities regarding human existential questions such as re-establishing and
preserving a sense of stability in the process of identity formation, or the potential for
truth in a representation. Such statements are by far the weightiest presence in almost
all of his meditations on the subject, and can sometimes leave an impression of puerile
idealism. Though these may, in themselves, be more features of a personal moral
stance than of any substantial theoretical position on film, they have nevertheless been
instrumental in the development of a personal film language, of which a true caring
for the medium is a constitutive part.

Wenders' reference, when explaining his motivations for making films, to Balázs'
phenomenological formulation of cinema's responsibility to show things 'as they are'
suggests that he perceives an intimate bond to exist between the aesthetic fundamentals
of his cinema and the fundamental aesthetic and technical nature of the cinematic
medium. In his films, this connection manifests itself in the use of the film image
– which, like photographic images, permits a maximum possible optical similarity
to the appearance of material phenomena in the representation – and of sound

– always an attribute of a material phenomenon, but which can exist independently of a corresponding visual referent – as the chief information transmitting devices. Significantly, there is no more to film than image and sound, if one is talking about film's fundamental properties (the same can be said of all audio-visual media).

A further relevant technical and aesthetic characteristic inherent to film (as a descendent of photography) is that it is a recording art or medium (unlike film and photography, not all audio-visual media can be considered to perform recording functions).[1] As records of the appearance of material phenomena, film images and sound, once recorded, can persist and be reviewed repeatedly over an extended period of time, making themselves available for viewing even when the recorded subject no longer exists in the same form. Wenders makes clear the relevance of this characteristic for his motivations in making films, and describes film's ability to assert the existence of material phenomena using moral terms.[2]

These inherent characteristics, however, have not alone been responsible for raising film (and the electronic media) to the most important, most popular, most influential, and most commercialised art form. Film, in the purely technical sense of the word, has had only little to do with cinema's historical success as a leisure activity among the broader public: it is merely the technical basis of the medium. A scientific film, perhaps, can be said to benefit alone from the technical characteristics of film as an adequately developed recording technology. It is nevertheless these characteristics, the primary aesthetic and technical characteristics of film, which Wenders evokes in his reference to Balázs above, on which the basis of his own cinema, and the higher purposes he ascribes to it, rest.

But Wenders' oeuvre is much more than a collection of recordings, an archive of images and sounds. Meaning can become attached to any film through its context. Although, for instance, Andy Warhol's film *Sleep* (1964) shows nothing more than a sleeping man for six hours, the film is considered an artistic rather than a scientific study (which it could equally be considered if the film appeared in a scientific context). Had a scientist made *Sleep* for scientific purposes, one would never consider evaluating its power of expression. A. L. Rees would have never considered the film to be a 'parody of the trance film', or remarked that we do not see the man's dreams.[3] Similarly, Wenders would perhaps never have described the Lumières' film *L'arriveé d'un train en gare*, as 'a moment of truth'[4] even though it was, in the very highest degree, a product and object of scientific research. The train, the subject of the film, is not the object of research here (as in a scientific film), but the film itself. The difference lies in the context and in the intervention of the directors that caused the film to be made.

Wenders' film *Silver City* goes one step further than Warhol's *Sleep* in this sense, because it has an audio track that is unrelated to the visuals. Beyond the universal necessity of selecting, framing, and timing a shot in film, music and visual effects have been added to the images of the film's material phenomena, the Munich suburbs. Equally, the ambient sound has either not been recorded, or it has been removed from the film. To the information both audio and visual tracks provide, and to the connotations these can give rise to, this combination adds a new abstract aspect, which is a product of the film-maker's active intervention in the representation, and an element of his aesthetic expression. Even though the audio and visual tracks are more than just physically separated in *Silver City*, the only concrete information the film offers the spectator is of a phenomenological nature (the blinking effect is a visual effect, not a piece of information): how the music sounds, what the Munich suburbs look like, and what is going on there at the time of filming are the subject of this film.

Silver City is far from being a documentary film, even though it consists of nothing more than a collection of audio and visual recordings. It is an experiment in filmic vision that makes allusions to biological vision as an ideal potential filmic vision. In the same way as the Lumières' film, *Silver City* is itself the object of examination here, rather than the subjects of the film's images. Defining exactly what, beyond the concrete information offered by the images and the sound, constitutes the 'more' in a film such as *Silver City*, is the job of the critics, but we might make a few hypotheses: poetry, emotion, memory, atmosphere, visual stimulation, mood. All of these derive exclusively from the fundamental technical and aesthetic characteristics inherent to the filmic medium, for, as with the Lumières' film, there was no other input to this film. Only features inherent to the filmic medium are employed: sound and image in their unaltered, original form, albeit selected, recorded, processed and removed from the depicted reality (a prerequisite of all recording arts and media). This means that the material phenomena appearing in the film is, in accordance with Balázs' dictum, respected, left, as far as is technically possible in film, unaltered (including the music).

Wenders' moral perspective regarding the function and responsibilities of cinema and film-makers seems to have been the driving force behind the development of his film language: a mode of expression that attempts to ensure that all material phenomena appear in his films self-assertively, in the existential sense. Sound and image are not only the sole component parts of film: due to the development of audio-visual recording technologies towards the ultimate goal of maximum accuracy in the representation, they potentiate a (moral *and* existential) respect for the appearance of material phenomena in film. Film and photography are Wenders' ideal tools.

But because Wenders' stance is, in its nature, a moral stance, he finds anything that causes a misbalance in this harmony between material phenomena and their representation in film a potential threat. *Paris, Texas*, for instance, thematises how commercial uses of images can degrade the subject of the images to serving an ulterior goal that has no natural relation to the depicted reality (in this case, images of women used for profit). Here, the gap between reality and representation (or the presence of intent in the making and use of the images other than the simple self-representation of the women in images) provokes, Wenders suggests, distortions in questions of identity. *Alice in the Cities* makes the same suggestion in connection with commercial images in general and, in particular, in connection with a televisual aesthetic. Similar claims are made by Wenders in countless written texts and interviews.

In this respect, Wenders' most consistently vehement attacks concern story in film, by which he effectively mounts a challenge on almost the whole history of narrative cinema. Paradoxically, filmic stories, as well as commercial images, whether filmic, photographic or electronic, also only exist in the form of sounds and images. But, although Wenders would disagree,[4] the commercial cinema does seem to have asserted its place in history as a natural storytelling medium. All visual media, including those pre-existing film, have always sought to appeal to the public through fantasy and fiction. The film script, the backbone of any conventional narrative film, descends, in form, from dramaturgy, theatrical production and the novel. In this respect, modern narrative cinema has simply adapted and developed pre-existing forms of narration. Still, in film, stories are told in sound and image, meaning that the potential to respect the appearance of physical reality remains.

Wenders begins to mistrust stories in film when they become more important than a film's images. This can be the case when, for instance, the story of a film pre-exists the film, also when the story is in the form of a film script. The pre-existence of the story means that the images have, above all, to fit into the story. Images may then no longer be chosen or appear on their own merit, but in support of an act of narration. This can compromise the value of the portrayed reality because the material phenomena present in the images of the film does not assert itself, but is instead the material adapted for, and consumed by, the story. As we have seen, Wenders' regular negative use of the term 'vampire' to describe stories alludes to this act of consumption.[5]

Also, the fact that a film must be assembled and thus manufactured during the editing process means that individual visual phenomena can be placed into a synthetic temporal and spatial relation with others, thereby diminishing their autonomy within the whole representation. Though it is precisely the case in *Silver City* that material phenomena are selected from various geographical locations at varying times, thus gaining a temporal relation (because of their succession) and a spatial relation (because of their succession, and their displacement from their actual locations) to one another in the film that do not correspond to nature, there is no sense of dramatic unity that suggests a connection between the individual episodes, other than their spatial and temporal proximity to one another within the framework of the film. The episodes remain autonomous, as does the music of the film, representing only themselves.

As he expresses through the figure of Homer in *Wings of Desire*, Wenders speculates that people need stories more than anything else. The core of Wenders' cinematic exploration has been the attempt to find ways of accommodating the demands of his spectatorship for story in film without compromising his own moral positions regarding the film image. The result is that he uses story only as a frame that can be drawn from any source, and, if a published literary work or script is used as a basis, then only to structure the films (*Wrong Movement*, *The American Friend*, *Paris, Texas*, *Wings of Desire*, *Until the End of the World*, *The End of Violence*, and *The Million Dollar Hotel*). In the absence of such sources, the given or found reality can be adapted (*Alice in the Cities*, *Kings of the Road*, *Nick's Film: Lightning Over Water*, *The State of Things*, and *Lisbon Story*). None of these films tell a story so assertive that the material phenomena appears in the films only to serve the telling of their stories. Usually, these framework stories are episodically structured to regularly interrupt and break up narrative development, and to avoid as much as possible the necessity of imposing artificial connections between unrelated time sequences and locations. Images (and sounds) are thus left to transmit most of the information in the films, thereby allowing the audio and visual tracks to 'speak' the language of material phenomena to their full potential.

As we have seen, Wenders' cinematic exploration represents a look back at the technical and aesthetic basis of film as an art form to identify in this what it can do best, and to assert this as a creative act: enabling the self-referential appearance of material phenomena in image and sound, as well as their presentation within the framework of a story. In this, one cannot say that Wenders follows any particular tradition. As stated at the outset of this study, it is difficult, bearing in mind the wide variety of genre and media Wenders works with, to find any unifying banner under which to summarise his work. To describe Wenders along the lines of a national cinema would be too restrictive. A German director he may be, but his films are, today, everything other than German. The expression 'European cinema' is also an insufficient description. And to attempt to label his work in terms of artistic movements is equally difficult and dissatisfying. Of course, terms such as 'pastiche' or 'fragmentation' may lead to relevant findings, yet to conclude such an investigation with an obligatory categorisation along the lines of modernist, postmodernist etc., as is the current trend in film criticism, may only provide the author/reader with a certain temporary thrill of summary certainty and accomplishment, a momentary feel-good factor, but this does not tell us much about the films themselves: the result is always the same unsatisfactory assertion of a director who, it seems, perpetually finds himself in the state of moving out of the modern towards the postmodern.

In keeping with the focus of this book on the one element that distinguishes film from the other arts – the capacity to both catch and freeze the flow of time and movement through space – what Wenders is perhaps most concerned with is the idea of memory. In what we may describe as a cult of the visual, Wenders believes in a cinema that can waken the spirit in things, that, through simple observation and representation, can narrate the flow of time in images as a memory of existence. In this, Wenders is unique in his consistency: one only has to consider the many direct references to figures such as Caspar David Friedrich (*Wrong Movement*), Jan Vermeer (*Until the End of the World*), Edward Hopper (*Reverse Angle: New York City, March 1982* and *The End of Violence*), or the photographer August Sander (*Wings of Desire*), to find confirmation of this fascination with observation and the observed, and with codes of representation of the visual world.

The presence of thickly layered narratives, Wenders knows, would only cloud this visuality, smothering and obscuring it with non-visual information that detracts meaning and attention from the visual experience, hindering the images in their job of narrating the visual itself as memory. Because this is so, a thin, skeletal narrative is required as a frame in which to present images. A frame in which there is no room for predetermined conclusions to events, narrative highlights or sensationalism. Also for this aspect there are ample clear references in Wenders' work to past inspirations: the direct references in *Alice in the Cities*, *Kings of the Road* and *Paris, Texas* to the figure of John Ford, whose narratives were a 'haven of rest and security'[6] for Wenders; the Japanese director Yazujiro Ozu, whose way of telling stories Wenders found so 'representational'; Italian director Michelangelo Antonioni, who was partly responsible for Wenders' experimentation with new image-making technologies, whose own films foreground the image and are practically void of story, and with whom Wenders, for the first and only time, co-directed a film; the figures of Homer, the blind poet who narrates the passing of time to his circle of listeners, and Walter Benjamin, whose written observations document a whole era in German and European history in *Wings of Desire*; the living memory of the Australian aboriginal 'Dream Time', a mythology of the creation of the world, handed down through the generations by word of mouth, keeping alive a sense of, or belief in, identity, and which is intimately linked to the land in which the people live, is presented as a cure for the illness of images that befalls the protagonists in *Until the End of the World*; and, lastly, Wenders' early appropriation of the road movie genre, in which movement through time is the sole generator of narrative progression along the never-ending celluloid highway. His most recent works – two documentary films on 'forgotten' musicians (*Buena Vista Social Club* and *Ode to Cologne – A Rock 'n' Roll Film*[7]), show a distinct shift towards the further separation and autonomy of the fundamental elements of film, and towards the concept of image as memory. And, considering the soundtrack and overall musical background to *The Million Dollar Hotel*, this shift reveals that Wenders is perhaps more confident than ever before about the direction this road has taken, and will take in the future.

NOTES

INTRODUCTION

1   Wim Wenders (1992) *The Logic of Images: Essays and Conversations*. London: Faber and Faber, p. 1.

2   Wim Wenders (1993) *Die Logik der Bilder: Essays und Gespräche*. Frankfurt am Main: Verlag der Autoren, p. 52.

3   Norbert Grob (1991) *Wim Wenders*. Berlin: Edition Filme, p. 162.

4   Wenders, *The Logic of Images*, p. 52.

5   *Ibid.*, p. 53.

6   *Ibid.*, p. 59.

7   *Ibid.*, p. 1.

8   Wim Wenders (1991) *Emotion Pictures: Reflections on the Cinema*. London: Faber and Faber, p. 19.

9   *Ibid.*, p. 35.

10 Frieda Grafe in Peter Jansen and Wolfram Schütte (eds) (1992) *Wim Wenders*. Munich and Vienna: Carl Hanser Verlag, p. 8.

11 Frank Schnelle (1993) 'In weiter Ferne, so nah', in *epd Film*, 09, p. 69.

12 *Ibid.*

13 Wenders, *The Logic of Images*, p. 59.

14 Wenders in Edgar Reitz (1995) *Bilder in Bewegung: Essays; Gespräche zum Kino*. Hamburg: Rowolt Taschenbuch Verlag, p. 192: 'Actually, I'm a documentary film-maker who tries to tell stories, but who wants to preserve something he has discovered in these stories.'

15 Reitz proposed a complete renewal of film and cinema including film structure, film form and even cinema architecture. For more information see Reitz (1984) *Liebe zum Kino: Utopien und Gedanken zum Autorenfilm 1962–1983*, 7–32.

16 David A. Cook (1990) *A History of Narrative Film* (Second Edition). London and New York: Emery University Press, p. 865.

17 Thomas Elsaesser (1989) *New German Cinema: A History*. New Jersey: Rutgers University Press, p. 134.

18 Cook, *A History of Narrative Film*, p. 858.

19 Wenders, *Emotion Pictures*, pp. 93–9.

20 *Ibid.*, p. 94.

21 Wenders, *The Logic of Images*, p. 19.

22 *Ibid.*

23 Wenders, *Emotion Pictures*, p. 29.

24 Cook, *A History of Narrative Film*, p. 480.

25 Elsaesser, *New German Cinema*, p. 136.

26 Wenders, *Emotion Pictures*, p. 124.

27 *Ibid.*, p. 126.

28 Robert Phillip Kolker and Peter Beicken (1993) *The Films of Wim Wenders: Cinema as Vision and Desire*. Cambridge: Cambridge University Press, p. 23.

29 Wenders, *The Logic of Images*, p. 47.

30 Kolker & Beicken, *The Films of Wim Wenders*, p. 39.

31 Wenders, *Emotion Pictures*, p. 115.

32 Wenders includes this scene in *Nick's Film: Lightning over Water*.

33 Wenders, *Emotion Pictures*, p. 104.

34 See Alexander Graf (1998) 'Videotechnik und die Suche nach dem Wahrhaftigen Bild: Zur Zusammenarbeit Antonionis und Wenders', in Volker Roloff, Schanze, Scheunemann (eds) *Europäische Kinokunst im Zeitalzer des Fernsehens*. Munich: Wilhelm Fink Verlag, pp. 383–91.

35 Wenders, *The Logic of Images*, p. 60.

36 Quoted in Filippo D'Angelo (1994) *Wim Wenders*. Milan: Editrice Il Castoro, p. 7.

37 Wenders, *The Logic of Images*, p. 95.

38 D'Angelo, *Wim Wenders*, p. 154.

39 Wenders, *The Logic of Images*, p. 20.

40 *The State of Things*.

41 Quoted in Grob, *Wim Wenders*, p. 264.

42 Quoted in Jan Dawson (1979) *Wim Wenders*. New York: Zoetrope, p. 10.

CHAPTER ONE

1 Wim Wenders (1997) *The Act of Seeing: Essays and Conversations*. London: Faber and Faber, p. 93.

2 Robert Bresson (1980) *Noten zum Kinomatographischen*. Munich: Carl Hanser Verlag, p. 21.

3 Edgar Morin (1958) *Der Mensch und das Kino: eine anthropologische Untersuchung*. Stuttgart: Klett Verlag, p. 68.

4 Reinhold Rauh (1990) *Wim Wenders und seine Filme*. Munich: Wilhelm Heyne Verlag, p. 125.

5 Wenders informs us that, unfortunately, most of this film has been lost.

6 Grob, *Wim Wenders*, p. 38.

7 Siegfried Kracauer (1965) *Theory of Film: The Redemption of Physical Reality*. New York: Oxford University Press, p. 27.

8 *Ibid.*, p. 63.

9 Pier Paulo Pasolini (1982) *Ketzerfahrungen 'Empirismo eretico'*. Frankfurt am Main: Ullstein, p. 219.

10 *Ibid.*, pp. 119–20.

11 Wenders, *The Logic of Images*, p. 19.

12 *Ibid.*, p. 1.

13 *Ibid.*, p. 2.

14 *Ibid.*, pp. 1–2.

15 Wenders in D'Angelo, *Wim Wenders*, p. 90.

16 Rauh, *Wim Wenders und seine Filme,* p. 39.

17 Peter Buchka (1983) *Augen kann man nicht kaufen: Wim Wenders und seine Filme*. Munich: Carl Hanser Verlag, p. 108.

18 *Ibid.*

19 Pasolini, *Ketzerfahrungen 'Empirismo eretico',* p. 226.

20 See sections on *Alice in the Cities* and *Wings of Desire* in this book.

21 André Bazin (1975:) *Was ist Kino? Bausteine zur Theorie des Films*. Köln: DuMont Schauberg Verlag, p. 68.

22 Wenders, *The Logic of Images*, p. 5.

23 Wenders, *The Act of Seeing*, p. 47.

24 Wenders, *The Logic of Images*, p. 60.

25 Wenders, *The Act of Seeing*, p. 68.

26 *Ibid.*

27 Buchka, *Augen kann man nicht kaufen,* p. 112.

28 Wenders, *The Logic of Images*, pp. 25–6. (Here, I have translated Godard's spoken text directly as the English text is unclear).

29 It is interesting to note that Wenders has regularly produced and directed advertising films for television, beginning with a film for the domestic appliances manufacturer Ariston in 1995, and for the *Deutsche Bundesbahn* in 1999. He has also appeared in a television advertisement for the credit company American Express. Wenders explains in interview in the colour supplement *Sette* to the Italian newspaper *Corriere della Sera* No. 28, 1995, that he accepted the advertising engagement with Ariston out of 'curiosity'.

30 Wenders, *The Act of Seeing*, p. 31.

31 Wenders, *Emotion Pictures*, p. 120.

32 *Ibid.*

33 Wenders, *The Logic of Images*, p. 22.

34 *Ibid.*

35 *Ibid.*

36 John Ellis (1992) *Visible Fictions: Cinema; Television; Video*. London and New York: Routledge, p. 240.

37 Kracauer, *Theory of Film,* p. 167.

38 Ellis, *Visible Fictions,* p. 236.

39 Wenders, *The Logic of Images*, p. 48.

40 Elliss, *Visible Fictions,* pp. 226–7.

41 Wim Wenders (1993) *Una Volta*. Rome: Edizioni Socrates, p. 387.

42 Ellis, *Visible Fictions,* p. 239.

43 *Ibid.*, p. 227.

44 Wenders, *The Logic of Images*, pp. 87–8.

CHAPTER TWO

1 Wenders, *The Logic of Images*, p. 53.

2 Kracauer, *Theory of Film,* p. 77.

3 Wenders, *The Act of Seeing*, p. 104.

4   Wenders, *The Logic of Images*, p. 4.

5   Wenders, *The Act of Seeing*, p. 108.

6   *Ibid.*, pp. 50–1.

7   Wenders, *The Logic of Images*, p. 8.

8   *Ibid.*, p. 7.

9   *Ibid.*, p. 18.

10 *Ibid.*, p. 53.

11 Wenders, *The Act of Seeing*, p. 107.

12 Wenders, *The Logic of Images*, pp. 21–2.

13 Grob, *Wim Wenders*, p. 14.

14 Wenders, *The Logic of Images*, p. 21.

15 *Ibid.*, p. 45.

16 Wenders in Edgar Reitz (1995) *Bilder in Bewegung: Gespräche zum Kino*. Hamburg: Rowolt Taschenbuch Verlag, p. 191.

17 Grob, *Wim Wenders*, p. 219. Grob does not specify his source.

18 Kracauer, *Theory of Film*, p. 245–6.

19 Jansen & Schütte, *Wim Wenders*, p. 44.

20 D'Angelo, *Wim Wenders*, p. 35.

21 Wenders, *The Act of Seeing*, p. 49.

22 *Ibid.*, p. 4.

23 Wenders, *The Logic of Images*, p. 101.

24 Kolker and Beicken, *The Films of Wim Wenders*, p. 47. (Though Ripley seems to conform to this idea, he attempts to prevent Jonathan's involvement in the crimes. It is rather the character Raoul Minot (Gerard Blain) who directly approaches Jonathan regarding the murders.)

25 D'Angelo, *Wim Wenders*, p. 93.

26 Rauh, *Wim Wenders und seine Filme*, p. 66.

27 D'Angelo, *Wim Wenders*, p. 94.

28 Kracauer, *Theory of Film*, p. 253.

29 Wenders, *The Logic of Images*, p. 1.

30 Wenders (1975) 'Interview with Tony Rayns', *Sight and Sound*, 44, 1, p. 5.

31 Wenders, *The Logic of Images*, p. 4. (This sequence lasts only 4': 46" in the 'Atlas Film Werkausgabe' version, from 1:03:34 – 1:08:20.)

32 The New Shorter Oxford English Dictionary defines an episode as: 'A scene or digression complete in itself but forming part of a continuous narrative.'

33 Pasolini, *Ketzerfahrungen 'Empirismo eretico'*, p. 221.

34 Jointly directed by Wenders and Michelangelo Antonioni.

35 Grob, *Wim Wenders*, p. 78.

36 Wenders, *The Logic of Images*, p. 53.

37 Kolker & Beicken, *The Films of Wim Wenders*, p. 5.

38 D'Angelo, *Wim Wenders*, p. 39.

39 Wenders, *The Logic of Images*, p. 46.

40 Wenders in Reitz, *Bilder in Bewegung*, p. 192.

41 See Roger F. Cook & Gerd Gemünden (eds) (1997) *The Cinema of Wim Wenders: Image, Narrative and the Postmodern Condition*. Detroit: Wayne State University Press, pp. 138–9.

42 Grob, *Wim Wenders*, p. 79.

43 Jean Paul Sartre (1987) *Nausea*. London: Penguin, pp. 61–2.

Germanic Review, 66, p. 38.

68 Kolker & Beicken, *The Films of Wim Wenders,* p. 4.

69 Wenders, *The Logic of Images*, p. 112.

70 *Ibid.*, p. 50.

71 Kolker & Beicken, *The Films of Wim Wenders,* p. 150–1.

72 Caldwell & Rea, 'Handke's and Wenders' *Wings of Desire*', p. 51.

73 Wenders, *The Logic of Images*, p. 112.

74 *Ibid.*, p. 44.

75 *Ibid.*, p. 112.

76 Wim Wenders & Peter Handke (1990) *Der Himmel über Berlin: ein Filmbuch.* Frankfurt an Main: Suhrkamp Verlag, p. 30.

77 *Ibid.*, p. 57.

78 Cook, 'Angels, Fiction and History in Berlin', p. 45.

79 Wim Wenders (1988–89) Interview with Katherine Dieckmann, *Sight and Sound*, 42, p. 6.

80 Wenders, *The Logic of Images*, p. 19.

81 Handke, *A Moment of True Feeling*, pp. 63–5.

82 Edward Plater (1992) states that emphasis here is placed on the storytelling capabilities of the visual image rather than the word.

83 Derek Malcolm in the online version of *Screen International*, 10th February 2000 (www. screendaily.com).

84 Merten Worthmann in *Die Zeit*, 3 February 2000, p. 41.

85 Elvis Mitchell in *The New York Times Online*, 2nd February 2001 (www.nytimes.com).

86 David Stratton in *Variety's* online edition, 10th February 2000 (www.variety.com).

87 One could say, however, that the hotel appears as a main protagonist: this view is supported because the camera almost never leaves the hotel, and the 'Million Dollar Hotel' appears in the cast credits immediately after Milla Jovovich.

88 Wenders in the Australian online publication www.abc.net.au.

89 Jansen and Schütte, *Wim Wenders*, p. 59.

90 Wenders in *Reverse Angle New York City, March 1982*.

91 Wenders, *The Act of Seeing*, p. 46.

92 Wim Wenders (1995b) *Lisbon Story* (film script). Mario Sesti (ed.) Milan: Ubulibri, p. 14.

93 See Mast, Cohen & Braudy, *Film Theory and Criticism,* pp. 317–19.

94 Ruttmann in Jeanpaul Goergen (ed.) (1989) *Walter Ruttmann: Eine Dokumentation.* Berlin: Freunde der deutschen Kinemathek, p. 83.

95 Elizabeth Weis & John Belton (eds) (1985) *Film Sound: Theory and Practice.* New York: Columbia University Press, pp. 116–17.

96 Belton in Mast, Cohen & Braudy, *Film Theory and Criticism*, p. 325.

97 Here and in other films (*Summer in the City, Alice in the Cities, Wings of Desire*), the band members appear performing their own music, hence the synchronisation.

98 See Wenders & Handke, *Der Himmel über Berlin*, pp. 8–17.

99 Wenders, *Emotion Pictures*, p. 50.

100 Weis & Belton, *Film Sound*, p. 116.

101 Near the end of the film, Teresa describes the music, which is audible in the background, and the river, which is faintly visible in the haze, as 'more or less the same thing'.

102 Wenders, *Lisbon Story*, p. 64 and p. 23.

103 Weis & Belton, *Film Sound*, p. 116.

104 Dziga Vertov in Pietro Montani (1975) *Vertov*. Milan: Editrice Il Castoro, no. 16, April, pp. 5–6.
105 *Ibid.*
106 Weis & Belton, *Film Sound*, p. 84.

CONCLUSION

1   Live television, for instance, does not necessarily perform a recording function.
2   Wenders refers to the act of filming as a 'heroic' act, and describes the film camera as a weapon against the 'misery' of the disappearance of things.
3   A. L. Rees (1999) *A History of Experimental Film and Video: From the Canonical Avant-garde to Contemporary British Practice*. London: BFI, p. 69.
4   Wenders, *Emotion Pictures*, pp. 51–9.
5   Wenders, *The Logic of Images*, p. 53.
6   Wenders in Kolker and Beicken, *The Films of Wim Wenders*, p. 39.
7   German title: *Viel Passiert – Der BAP Film*, premiered at the Berlin Film Festival, February 2002.

FILMOGRAPHY

Abbreviations:
d – director; *p* – producer; *c* – camera; *sc* – script; *ed* – editor; *m* – music; *sd* – sound ; *lp* – leading players

Schauplätze (*Locations*, 1967)
d, p, c, sc, ed: Wim Wenders. *m*: The Rolling Stones. 10 min., l6mm, b/w.
No prints exist; the only two surviving shots appear at the beginning of *Same Player Shoots Again.*

Same Player Shoots Again (1967)
d, p, c, sc, ed: Wim Wenders. 12 min., l6mm, b/w (differently tinted).

Silver City (1968)
d, p, c, sc, ed: Wim Wenders. 25 min., l6mm, col.

Alabama: 2000 Light Years From Home (1968)
d, sc, ed: Wim Wenders. *p*: Hochschule für Fernsehen und Film, Munich. *c*: Robby Müller. *m*: The Rolling Stones, Jimi Hendrix, Bob Dylan, John Coltrane. 21 min., 35mm, b/w. *lp*: Paul Lys, Werner Schroeter, Peter Kaiser, Muriel Schrat, Christian Friedel.

Polizeifilm (*Police Film*, 1969)
d, c, ed: Wim Wenders. *p*: Bayerischer Rundfunk, Munich. *sc*: Albrecht Göschel, Wim Wenders. 11 min., l6mm, b/w. *lp*: Jimmy Vogler, Kasimir Esser.

3 amerikanische LP's (*3 American LPs*, 1969)
d, ed, sd: Wim Wenders. *p*: Hessischer Rundfunk, Frankfurt. *sc*: Peter Handke. *m*: Van Morrison, Creedence Clearwater Revival, Harvey Mandel. 13 min., l6mm, col. *lp*: Wim Wenders, Peter Handke.

Summer in the City (Dedicated to The Kinks) (1970)

d, *sc*: Wim Wenders. *p*: Hochschule für Film und Fernsehen, Munich. *c*: Robby Müller. *ed*: Peter Przygodda. *m*: The Kinks, Lovin' Spoonful, Chuck Berry, Gene Vincent, The Troggs. 145 min. (first version), 116 min. (second version), l6mm, b/w. *lp*: Hans Zischler (Hans), Edda Köchl (friend in Munich), Libgart Schwarz (girlfriend in Berlin), Maria Bardischewski (friend in Berlin), Wim Wenders (friend at pool hall).

Die Angst des Tormanns beim Elfmeter (*The Goalkeeper's Fear of the Penalty Kick*, 1971)

d: Wim Wenders. *p*: Filmverlag der Autoren, Munich; Telefilm AG, Wien; Westdeutscher Rundfunk Cologne. *sc*: Wim Wenders, after the novel by Peter Handke. *c*: Robby Müller. *ed*: Peter Przygodda. *sd*: Rainer Lorenz, Martin Müller. *m*: Jürgen Knieper. 100 min., 35mm, col. *lp*: Arthur Brauss (Josef Bloch), Erika Pluhar (Gloria), Kai Fischer (Hertha Gabler), Libgart Schwarz (Anna), Maria Bardischewski (Maria), Rüdiger Vogler (village idiot), Wim Wenders (walks through Vienna bus station).

Der Scharlachrote Buchstabe (*The Scarlet Letter*, 1972)

d: Wim Wenders. *p*: Filmverlag der Autoren, Munich; Westdeutscher Rundfunk, Cologne; Elias Querejeta, Madrid. *sc*: Wim Wenders, Bernardo Fernandez, after the script by Tankred Dorst and Ursula Ehler, *Der Herr klagt über sein Volk in der Wildnis Amerika,* based on the novel *The Scarlet Letter* by Nathaniel Hawthorne. *c*: Robby Müller. *ed*: Peter Przygodda. *sd*: Christian Schubert. *m*: Jürgen Knieper. 90 min., 35mm, col. *lp*: Senta Berger (Hester Prynne), Hans Christian Blech (Chillingworth), Lou Castel (Dimmesdale), Yella Rottländer (Pearl), William Layton (Bellingham).

Alice in den Städten (*Alice in the Cities*, 1974)

d: Wim Wenders. *p*: Filmverlag der Autoren, Munich; Westdeutscher Rundfunk, Cologne. *sc*: Wim Wenders, Veith von Fürstenburg. *c*: Robby Müller. *ed*: Peter Przygodda. *sd*: Martin Müller, Paul Schöler. *m*: Can, Chuck Berry, Canned Heat, Deep Purple, Count Five, The Stories. 110 min., l6mm, b/w. *lp*: Rüdiger Vogler (Philip Winter), Yella Rottländer (Alice), Lisa Kreuzer (Lisa van Damm), Edda Köchl (Angela, girlfriend in New York), Wim Wenders (man standing at jukebox).

Aus der Familie der Panzerechsen/Die Insel (*The Crocodile Family/The Island*, 1974)

d: Wim Wenders. *p*: Bavaria, Munich, as part of the television series *Ein Haus für alle*. *sc*: Philippe Pilloid. *c*: Michael Ballhaus. *ed*: Lilian Seng. *sd*: Armin Münch, Walter Hutterer. *m*: Arpad Bondy. 50 min., l6mm, col. *lp*: Katja Wulff (Ute), Lisa Kreuzer (social worker), Thomas Braut (director of the school), Marquard Bohm (visitor at the zoo), Nicholas Brieder (father), Hans-Joachim Krietsch (psychologist), Helga Tomper (mother).

Falsche Bewegung (*Wrong Movement*, 1975)

d: Wim Wenders. *p*: Solaris Film, Munich; Westdeutscher Rundfunk, Cologne. *sc*: Peter Handke, freely adapted from Johann Wolfgang von Goethe's *Wilhelm Meisters Lehrjahre*. *c*: Robby Müller. *ed*: Peter Przygodda. *sd*: Martin Müller, Peter Kaiser, Paul Schöler. *m*: Jürgen Knieper. 104 min., 35mm, col. *lp*: Rüdiger Vogler (Wilhelm), Hanna Schygulla (Therese), Hans Christian Blech (Laertes), Nastassja Kinski (Mignon), Peter Kern (Landau), Ivan Desny (industrialist), Marianne Hoppe (mother), Lisa Kreuzer (Janine), Wim Wenders (man in dining car).

Im Lauf der Zeit (Kings of the Road, 1976)

d: Wim Wenders. *p*: Wim Wenders Produktion, Munich; Westdeutscher Rundfunk, Cologne. *sc*: Wim Wenders. *c*: Robby Müller. *ed*: Peter Przygodda. *sd*: Martin Müller, Bruno Bollhalder. *m*: Improved Sound Limited, Axel Linstädt. 176 min., 35mm, b/w. *lp*: Rüdiger Vogler (Bruno), Hans Zischler (Robert), Lisa Kreuzer (Pauline), Rudolf Schündler (father), Marquard Bohm (husband of the woman who committed suicide), Dieter Traier (Robert's friend from school), Wim Wenders (spectator at Pauline's theatre).

Der amerikanische Freund (The American Friend, 1977)

d: Wim Wenders. *p*: Road Movies, Berlin; Les Films du Losange Paris; Wim Wenders Produktion, Munich; Westdeutscher Rundfunk, Cologne. *sc*: Wim Wenders, after Patricia Highsmith's novel *Ripley's Game*. *c*: Robby Müller. *ed*: Peter Przygodda. *sd*: Martin Müller, Peter Kaiser. *m*: Jürgen Knieper. 123 min., 35mm, col. *lp*: Bruno Ganz (Jonathan Zimmermann), Dennis Hopper (Tom Ripley), Lisa Kreuzer (Marianne Zimmermann), Gerard Blain (Raoul Minôt), Nicholas Ray (Derwatt), Samuel Fuller (the American mafioso), Wim Wenders (figure wrapped in plaster bandages in ambulance).

Nick's Film: Lightning Over Water (1980)

d: Nicholas Ray, Wim Wenders. *p*: Road Movies, Berlin; Wim Wenders Produktion, Berlin; Viking-Film, Stockholm *sc*: Wim Wenders. *c*: Edward Lachmann, Martin Schifer (film), Tom Farell (video). *ed*: Peter Przygodda (first version), Wim Wenders (second version). *sd*: Martin Müller, Maryte Kavahauskas, Gary Steele. *m*: Ronee Blakely. 116 min. (first version), 90 min. (second version), 35mm, col. *lp*: Nicholas Ray, Wim Wenders, Susan Ray, Timothy Ray, Tom Farrell, Ronee Blakely, Gerry Bauman, Pierre Cottrell, Stephan Czapsky, Becky Johnston, Tom Kaufmann, Craig Nelson, Pat Kirck, Edward Lachmann, Maryte Kavahauskas, Martin Müller, Martin Schifer, Chris Sievernich.

Hammett (1982)

d: Wim Wenders. *p*: Zoetrope Studios, San Francisco; Orion Pictures, New York. *sc*: Ross Thomas, Dennis O'Flaherty, Thomas Pope, Joe Gores, after the novel by Joe Gores. *c*: Philip Lathrop, Joseph Biroc. *ed*: Barry Malkin, Marc Laub, Rober Q. Lovett, Randy Roberts, Andrew London. *sd*: James Webb Jr., Richard Goodman. *m*: John Barry. 94 min., 35mm, col. *lp*: Frederic Forrest (Hammett), Peter Boyle (Jimmy Ryan), Marilu Henner (Kit Conger, Sue Alabama), Roy Kinnear (Eddie Hagedorn), Elisha Cook Jr. (cab driver), Lydia Lei (Chrystal Ling), R. G. Annstrong (O'Mara), Richard Bradford (Tom Bradford).

Der Stand der Dinge (The State of Things, 1982)

d: Wim Wenders. *p*: Road Movies, Berlin; Wim Wenders Produktion, Berlin; Gray City Inc., New York; Project Filmproduktion, Munich; Zweites Deutsches Fernsehen, Mainz; Pan Films, Paris; Musidora, Madrid; Film International, Rotterdam; Artificial Eye, London. *sc*: Wim Wenders, Robert Kramer. *c*: Henri Alekan, Martin Schifer, Fred Murphy. *ed*: Barbara von Weitershausen, Peter Przygodda. *sd*: Maryte Kavahauskas, Martin Müller. *m*: Jürgen Knieper. 120 min., 35mm, b/w. *lp*: Patrick Bauchau (Friedrich Munro), Isabelle Weingarten (Anna), Rebecca Pauly (Joan), Jeffrey Kime (Mark), Geoffrey Carey (Robert), Camilla Mora (Julia), Alexandra Auder (Jane), Paul Getty III (Dennis), Viva Auder (Kate).

Reverse Angle: New York City, March 1982 (1982)

d, sc: Wim Wenders. *p*: Gray City, New York; Antenne 2, Paris. *c*: Liza Rinsler. *ed*: Jon Neuburger. *sd*: Maryte Kavahauskas. *m*: Public Image Limited, Echo and the Bunnymen, Martha and the Muffins, The Del Byzanteens, Allen Goorwitz. 17 min., 16mm, col. *lp*: Wim Wenders, Isabelle Weingarten, Tony Richardson, Louis Malle, Francis Ford Coppola.

Chambre 666: Cannes May '82 (1982)

d, sc: Wim Wenders. *p*: Gray City, New York; Antenne 2, Paris. *c*: Agnes Godard. *ed*: Chantal de Vismes. *sd*: Jean-Paul Mugel. *m*: Jürgen Knieper, Berhard Herrmann. 45 min., 16mm, col. *lp*: Jean-Luc Godard, Paul Morrissey, Mike de Leon, Monte Hellman, Romain Goupil, Susan Seidelman, Noel Simsolo, Rainer Werner Fassbinder, Werner Herzog, Robert Kramer, Ana Carolina, Mahroun Baghbadi, Steven Spielberg, Michelangelo Antonioni, Wim Wenders, Yilmaz Goney (voice only).

Docu Drama (1984)

d: Wim Wenders. *p*: Wenders, Ronee Blakley. 100 min. *lp*: Wim Wenders, Ronee Blakely, Scarlet Rivera, Old Dog Band, Eulogy Band.

Paris, Texas (1984)

d: Wim Wenders. *p*: Road Movies, Berlin; Argos Films, Paris; Westdeutscher Rundfunk, Cologne; Channel 4, London; Project Filmproduktion im Filmverlag der Autoren, Munich. *sc*: Sam Shepard. *c*: Robby Müller. *ed*: Peter Przygodda. *sd*: Jean-Paul Mugel. *m*: Ry Cooder. 145 min., 35mm, col. *lp*: Harry Dean Stanton (Travis), Nastassja Kinski (Jane), Dean Stockwell (Walt), Aurore Clement (Anne), Hunter Carson (Hunter), Bernhard Wicki (Dr. Ulmer), John Lurie (Slater), Sam Berry (man at gas station).

Tokyo Ga (1985)

d, sc: Wim Wenders. *p*: Wim Wenders Produktion, Berlin; Gray City, New York; Chris Sievernich Produktion, Berlin; Westdeutscher Rundfunk, Cologne. *c*: Edward Lachman. *ed*: Wim Wenders, Solveig Dommartin, John Neuburger. *sd*: Hartmut Eichgrün. *m*: Dick Tracy, Loorie Petitgrand, Mechne Mamecier, Chico Rojo Ortega. 92 min., 16mm, col. *lp*: Chishu Ryu, Yuhara Atsuta, Werner Herzog.

Der Himmel über Berlin (*Wings of Desire*, 1987)

d: Wim Wenders. *p*: Road Movies, Berlin; Argos Films, Paris; Westdeutscher Rundfunk, Cologne. *sc*: Wim Wenders, Peter Handke, Richard Reitinger. *c*: Henri Alekan. *ed*: Peter Przygodda. *sd*: Jean–Paul Mugel, Axel Arit. *m*: Jürgen Knieper, Laurent Petitgrand, Laurie Anderson, Crime and the City Solution, Nick Cave and the Bad Seeds, Sprung aus den Wolken, Tuxedomoon, Minimal Compact. 126 min., 35mm, b/w and col. *lp*: Bruno Ganz (Damiel), Solveig Dommartin (Marion), Otto Sander (Cassiel), Curt Bois (Homer), Peter Falk (Peter Falk), Hans Martin Stier, Elmar Wilms, Sigurd Rachman, Beatriz Mankowski, Lajos Kovacs.

Aufzeichnungen zu Kleidern und Städten (*Notes on Cities and Clothes*, 1989)

d, sc: Wim Wenders. *p*: Road Movies. *c*: Robby Müller, Muriel Edelstein, Uli Kudicke, Wim Wenders, Musatocki Nakajima, Masasai Chikamori. *ed*: Dominique Auvray, Lenie Saviette, Anne Schnee. 90 min., 35mm and video, col.

Bis ans Ende der Welt (*Until the End of the World*, 1991)

d: Wim Wenders. *p*: Road Movies, Berlin; Argos Film; Village Roadshow. *sc*: Peter Carvey, Wim Wenders, after an idea by Wim Wenders and Solveig Dommartin. *c*: Robby Müller. *ed*: Peter Przygodda. *m*: Graeme Revell, David Darling, Talking Heads, REM, Lou Reed, Nick Cave, Crime and the City Solution, T Bone Burnett, Can, Nench Cherry, Depeche Mode, Robbie Robertson & Blue Nile, The Kinks, Elvis Costello, Daniel Lanois, Peter Gabriel, U2, Patti & Fred Smith, Jane Siberry, k. d. lang. 179 min. (Europe), 157 min. (U.S.), 35mm, col. *lp*: Solveig Dommartin (Claire), William Hurt (Sam Farber), Jeanne Moreau (Edith Farber) Max von Sydow (Henry Farber), Chick Ortega (Chico), Sam Neill (Eugene Fitzpatrick), Rüdiger Vogler (Phillip Winter), Eddy Mitchell (Raymond), Ernie Dingo (Burt), Elena Smirnowa (Krasikowa), Ryu Chishu (Mr. Mori), Allen Garfield (Bernie), Lois Chiles (Elsa), David Gulpilil (David), Charlie McMahon (Buzzer), Justine Saunders (Maisie), Jimmy Little (Peter), Kylie Belling (Lydia), Rhoda Roberts (Ronda), Paul Livingston (Karl), Bart Willoughby (Ned).

Arisha, der Bär, und der steinerne Ring (*Arisha, the Bear, and the Stone Ring*, 1992)

d, sc: Wim Wenders. *p*: Road Movies. *c*: Jürgen Jürges. *ed*: Peter Przygodda. *m*: Nick Cave and the Bad Seeds, The House of Love, Crime and the City Solution, Ed Kuepper. 45 min., 35mm and video, col. *lp*: Rüdiger Vogler (Bear), Anna Vronskaya (woman), Arina Voznesenskaya (child), Wim Wenders (Santa Claus), Gong Rung Truong, Nam Ha Nguyen, Thi Hoa Nguyen (Vietnamese family).

In weiter Ferne, so nah (*Far Away, So Close*, 1993)

d: Wim Wenders. *p*: Road Movies; Tobis Filmkunst. *sc*: Wim Wenders, Ulrich Ziegler, Richard Reitinger. *ed*: Peter Przygodda *m*: U2, Crime and the City Solution, Jane Siberry, Laurie Anderson, Herbert Grönemeyer, Guy Chadwick and The House of Love, Lou Reed. 146 min., 35mm, col. and b/w. *lp*: Otto Sander (Cassiel), Bruno Ganz (Damiel), Nastassja Kinski (Raphaela), Martin Olbertz (dying man), Lou Reed, Michail Gorbatchov, Heinz Rührmann (Konrad), Horst Buchholz (Tony Baker), Rüdiger Vogler (Phillip Winter), Yella Rottländer (Winter's angel), Hanns Zischler (Dr. Becker), Solveig Dommartin (Marion), Willem Dafoe (Emit Flesti).

Lisbon Story (1994)

d, sc: Wim Wenders, *p*: Road Movies. *c*: Lisa Rinzler. *ed*: Peter Przygodda, Anne Schnee. *m*: Madredeus. *sd*: Jürgen Knieper. 105 min., 35mm, col. and b/w. *lp*: Rüdiger Vogler (Philip Winter), Patrick Bauchau (Friedrich Monroe), Ricardo Colares (Ricardo), Joe Ferreira (Ze'), Teresa Salgueiro (Teresa), Manoel De Oliveira.

Par Delà les Nuages (*Beyond the Clouds*, 1995)

d: Michelangelo Antonioni, Wim Wenders. *p*: Philippe Carcasonne, Stephane Tchal Gadjieff. *sc*: Tonino Guerra, Michelangelo Antonioni, Wim Wenders. *c*: Alfio Contini, Robby Müller. *ed*: Peter Przygodda, Lucian Segura. *m*: Lucio Dalla, Laurent Petitgrand, Van Morrison, U2. 113 min., 35mm, col. *lp*: Fanny Ardant (Patrizia), Chiara Caselli (Olga), Irene Jacob (young woman), John Malkovich (director), Sophie Marceau (young woman), Vincent Perrez (Niccolo), Jean Reno (Carlo), Kim Rossi Stuart (Silvano), Ines Sastre (Carmen), Peter Weller (Roberto), Marcello Mastroianni (painter), Jeanne Moreau (friend).

Die Gebrüder Skladanowski (*A Trick of the Light*, 1996)

d, sc: Wim Wenders (with the students of the HFF Munich: Carlos Alvarez. Sebastian Andrac, Sorin Dragoi, Peter Fuchs, Carsten Funche, Florian Gallenberger, Makun Hansen, Henrik Heckmann, Veit Helmer, German Kral, Björn Kurt, Bodo Lang, Matthias Lehinanri, Eva Munz, Stefan Puchner, Barbara Rohm, Britta Sauer, Marcus Schmidt, Alma Teodorescu). *p*: Wim Wenders Produktion, Hochschule für Fernsehen und Film, Munich, Veit Heliner Filmproduktion. *c*: Jürgen Jürges. *ed*: Peter Przygodda. *m*: Laurent Petigrand. 79 min., 35mm, col. and b/w. *lp*: Udo Kier (Max Skladanowski), Nadine Buttner (Gertrud Skladanowski), Christoph Merg (Eugen Skladanowski), Otto Kuhnle (Emil Skladanowski), Lucie Hürtgen Skladanowski.

Am Ende der Gewalt (*The End of Violence*, 1997)

d: Wim Wenders. *p*: Ciby Pictures, Road Movies, Kintop Pictures. *sc*: Nicholas Klein, Wim Wenders. *c*: Pasca Rabaud. *ed*: Peter Przygodda. *m*: Ry Cooder. *sd*: Jim Stuebe. 122 min., 35mm, col. *lp*: Bill Pullman (Mike Max), Andie MacDowell (Paige Stockard), Traci Lind (Cat), Gabriel Byrne (Ray Berm), Rosalind Chao (Claire), Pruitt Taylor Vince (Frank Cray), John Diehl (Lowell Lewis), Richard Cummings (Tyler), Chris Douridas (mechanic), Nicole Parker (Kenya).

Willie Nelson at the Teatro (1998)

d, sc: Wim Wenders. *p*: Road Movies. *c*: Phedon Papamichael. *ed*: Wim Wenders. *m*: Willie Nelson. *lp*: Willie Nelson, Emmy Lou Harris, Daniel Lanois, Bobbie Nelson, Mickey Raphael, Victor Idrizzo, Tony Mangurian, Brian Griffith, Aaron Embry.

Buena Vista Social Club (1999)

d: Wim Wenders. *p*: Road Movies, Kinotop Pictures, Arte. *c*: Jörg Widmer. Ed: Brian Johnson. *m*: Ry Cooder and Buena Vista Social Club (Ibrahim Ferrer, Rubén Gonzáles, Eliades Ochoa, Omara Portuondo, Compay Segundo). 100 min., Digibeta and digital Handycam (35mm blow-up), col. *lp*: Wim Wenders, Ry Cooder, Joachim Cooder, Ibrahim Ferrer, Rubén Gonzáles, Eliades Ochoa, Omara Portuondo, Compay Segundo.

The Million Dollar Hotel (1999)

d: Wim Wenders. *p*: Road Movies, Kinotop Pictures. *sc*: Nicholas Klein, Bono. *c*: Phedon Papamichael. *ed*: Tatjana S. Riegel. *m*: Bono, Brian Eno, U2. *sd*: Lee Orloff. 122 min. 35mm, col. *lp*: Jeremy Davies (Tom Tom), Milla Jovovich (Eloise), Mel Gibson (Skinner), Tim Roth (Izzy), Peter Stormare (Dixie), Jimmy Smits (Geronimo), Gloria Stuart (Jessica), Donal Logue (Best), Bud Cort (Shortie).

Viel Passiert – Der Bap Film (*Ode to Cologne: A Rock 'n' Roll Film*, 2001)

d: Wim Wenders. *p*: Road Movies, Westdeutscher Rundfunk, Screenworks Köln, BAP Travelling Tune Productions, *sc*: Wim Wenders. *m*: BAP. 96 min., Digibeta (35mm blow-up), col. *lp*: Marie Bäumer, Joachim Król, Willi Laschet, Wolf Biermann.

Twelve Miles to Trona (2002)

d, sc: Wim Wenders. p: Road Movies. c: Phedon Papamichael. ed: Mathilde Bonnefoy. m: The Eels. sd: Jörn Steinhoff. 10 min., col. lp: Charles Esten (Bill), Amber Tamblyn (Kate), In-Ah Lee (Nurse 1), Myriam Zschage (Nurse 2), Wim Wenders (Doctor 1), Pascal Leister (Doctor 2), Peggy Perrige (Old Kate).

BIBLIOGRAPHY

Antoccia, Luca (1994) *Il Viaggio nel Cinema di Wim Wenders*. Bari Edizioni: Dedalo.

Baier, Martin (1996) *Film, Video und HDTV: Die Audiovisionen des Wim Wenders*. Berlin: Köhler Verlag.

Bazin, André (1971) *What is Cinema?* Berkeley, Los Angeles: University of California Press.

Benjamin, Walter (1970) *Illuminations*. London: Jonathan Cape.

Bordwell, David and Kristin Thompson (1993) *Film Art: An Introduction*. University of Wisconsin: McGraw-Hill.

Bordwell, David, Janet Staiger and Kristin Thompson (1994) *The Classical Hollywood Cinema: Film Style and Modes of Production to 1960*. London: Routledge.

Bresson, Robert (1980) *Noten zum Kinomatographischen*. Munich: Carl Hanser Verlag.

Buchka, Peter (1983) *Augen kann man nicht kaufen: Wim Wenders und seine Filme*. Munich: Carl Hanser Verlag.

Caldwell, David and Paul W. Rea (1991) 'Handke's and Wenders' *Wings of Desire:* Transcending Postmodernism', *German Quarterly*, 64, Winter, pp. 46–60.

Cook, David A. (1990) *A History of Narrative Film* (Second Edition). London, and New York: Emery University.

Cook, Roger (1991) 'Angels, Fiction and History in Berlin: Wim Wenders' *Wings of Desire*', *The Germanic Review*, 66, pp. 34–47.

Cook, Roger F. and Gerd Gemünden (eds) (1997) *The Cinema of Wim Wenders: Image, Narrative and the Postmodern Condition*. Detroit: Wayne State University Press.

D'Angelo, Filippo (1994) *Wim Wenders*. Milan: Editrice Il Castoro.

Dawson, Jan (1979) *Wim Wenders*. New York: Zoetrope.

Di Marino, Bruno (ed.) (1995) *Wim Wenders*. Rome: Dino Audino Editore.

Eastthorpe, Anthony (ed.) (1993) *Contemporary Film Theory*. London and New York: Longman Critical Readers.

Ellis, John (1992) *Visible Fictions: Cinema; Television; Video*. London and New York: Routledge.

Elsaesser, Thomas (1989) *New German Cinema: A History*. New Jersey: Rutgers University Press.

Friedberg, Anne (1993) *Window Shopping: Cinema and the Postmodern*. Berkeley: University of California Press.

Gariazzo, Giuseppe, Roberto Lasagna and Saverio Zumbo (eds) (1997) *Wenders Story: Il Cinema, il Mito*. Alessandria: Edizioni Falsopiano.

Goergen, Jeanpaul (ed.) (1989) *Walter Ruttmann: Eine Dokumentation*. Berlin: Freunde der deutschen Kinemathek.

Graf, Alexander (1998) 'Videotechnik und die Suche nach dem Wahrhaftigen Bild: Zur Zusammenarbeit Antonionis und Wenders', in Volker Roloff, Helmut Schanze and Dietrich Scheunemann (eds) *Europäische Kinokunst im Zeitalter des Fernsehens*. Munich: Wilhelm Fink Verlag, pp. 383–91.

Grafe, Frieda (1992) 'Lob auf Wim Wenders' in Peter Jansen and Wolfram Schütte (eds.) (1992) *Wim Wenders*. Munich and Vienna: Carl Hanser Verlag, p. 7–14.

Grob, Norbert (1989) *Auf der Suche nach dem verlorenen Augenblick*. Berlin: Edition Filme.

_____ (1991) *Wim Wenders*. Berlin: Edition Filme.

Handke, Peter (1977) *A Moment of True Feeling*. New York: Farrar, Straus and Giroux.

Jansen, Peter and Wolfram Schütte (eds) (1992) *Wim Wenders*. Munich and Vienna: Carl Hanser Verlag.

Kolker, Robert Phillip and Peter Beicken (1993) *The Films of Wim Wenders: Cinema as Vision and Desire*. Cambridge: Cambridge University Press.

Kracauer, Siegfried (1965) *Theory of Film: The Redemption of Physical Reality*. New York: Oxford University Press.

Márquez, Gabriel García (1982) *One Hundred Years of Solitude*. London: Picador.

Mast, Gerald, Marshall Cohen and Leo Braudy (eds) (1992) *Film Theory and Criticism: Introductory Readings*. New York and Oxford: Oxford University Press.

Montani, Pietro (1975) *Vertov*. Milan: Editrice Il Castoro, pp. 5-6.

Morin, Edgar (1958) *Der Mensch und das Kino: eine anthropologische Untersuchung*. Stuttgart: Klett Verlag.

Mulvey, Laura (1975) 'Visual Pleasure and Narrative Cinema', *Screen* 16, 3, pp. 6–18.

Mundy, John (1999) *Popular Music on Screen: From Hollywood Musical to Music Video*. Manchester: Manchester University Press.

Orr, John (1993) *Cinema and Modernity*. Cambridge, Polity Press.

Pasolini, Pier Paolo (1982) *Ketzerfahrungen 'Empirismo eretico'*. Frankfurt am Main: Ullstein.

Plater, Edward M. V. (1992) 'The Storyteller in Wim Wenders' *Wings of Desire*', *Postscript*, 12, pp. 13–25.

Rauh, Reinhold (1990) *Wim Wenders und seine Filme*. Munich: Wilhelm Heyne Verlag.

Rees, A. L. (1999) *A History of Experimental Film and Video: From the Canonical Avant-garde to Contemporary British Practice*. London: BFI.

Reitz, Edgar (1984) *Liebe zum Kino: Utopien und Gedanken zum Autorenfilm 1962–1983*. Cologne: Verlag Köln.

_____ (1995) *Bilder in Bewegung: Gespräche zum Kino*. Hamburg: Rowolt Taschenbuch Verlag.

Russo, Maurizio (1997) *Wim Wenders: Prcezione visiva e conoscenza*. Genova: Le-Mani-Microarts Edizioni.

Sartre, Jean Paul (1987) *Nausea*. London: Penguin.

Schnelle, Frank (1993) 'In weiter Ferne, so nah', in *epd Film*, p. 9.

Weis, Elizabeth and John Belton (eds) (1985) *Film Sound: Theory and Practice*. New York: Columbia University Press.

Wenders, Wim (1975) Interview with Tony Raynes, *Sight and Sound*, 44, 1, pp. 5–6.

_____ (1984–85) Interview with Katherine Dieckmann, *Film Quarterly*, Winter, no. 38, 2 pp. 2–7.

_____ (1988–89) Interview with Katherine Dieckmann, *Sight and Sound*, 42, pp. 2–8.

_____ (1991) *Emotion Pictures: Reflections on the Cinema*. London: Faber and Faber.

_____ (1992) *The Logic of Images: Essays and Conversations*. London: Faber and Faber.

_____ (1993) *Die Logik der Bilder: Essays und Gespräche*. Frankfurt am Main: Verlag der Autoren.

_____ (1993) *Una Volta*. Rome: Edizioni Socrates.

____ (1995a) Interview, with Paolo Mereghetti in *Sette,* no. 28, 18 December, colour supplement to *Corriere della Sera*, pp. 40–4.

____ (1995b) *Lisbon Story* (film script). Mario Sesti (ed.) Milan: Ubulibri.

____ Wenders, Wim and Peter Handke (1990) *Der Himmel über Berlin: ein Filmbuch.* Frankfurt am Main: Suhrkamp Verlag.

____ (1997) *The Act of Seeing: Essays and Conversations.* London: Faber and Faber.

INDEX